# REFLECTIONS

*To my friend Pastor Greg Brewer*

*Phillip Michael Garner*

# REFLECTIONS

Seven Categories of Thought
for Today's Christians

Phillip Michael Garner

WIPF & STOCK · Eugene, Oregon

REFLECTIONS
Seven Categories of Thought for Today's Christians

Copyright © 2019 Phillip Michael Garner. All rights reserved. Except for brief quotations in critical publications or reviews, no part of this book may be reproduced in any manner without prior written permission from the publisher. Write: Permissions, Wipf and Stock Publishers, 199 W. 8th Ave., Suite 3, Eugene, OR 97401.

Wipf & Stock
An Imprint of Wipf and Stock Publishers
199 W. 8th Ave., Suite 3
Eugene, OR 97401

www.wipfandstock.com

PAPERBACK ISBN: 978-1-5326-9492-9
HARDCOVER ISBN: 978-1-5326-9493-6
EBOOK ISBN: 978-1-5326-9494-3

Manufactured in the U.S.A.                                   10/02/19

# Dedication

THE CONTENT OF THIS book was written while I've been living on Mactan Island in the Philippines. I initially shared the ideas in the following pages with my MTS students at The Institute for Global Outreach Developments International.

This book is dedicated to my parents, Darrell and Gerrie Garner, who are both in their eighties and live in Brentwood, Tennessee. My father's love language has always been expressed through his driving desire to provide for his family and ensure that none of us suffered lack. He is a skilled builder and accomplished artist. His work is always marked with the perfection of a meticulous nature.

My mother has an indomitable faith and provides a listening ear that has blessed all of my relatives. As a young girl she initially learned to play piano on a piece of wood with the keys of a piano painted on it. She took all three of my children to piano lessons for years.

I am the first person in our immediate family to make academic and intellectual pursuit a vocation. My parents have been supportive of this effort in a multiplicity of ways. My thoughts are far removed from our family's historical religious origins, but nevertheless the cathartic therapy of emotional religion benefited my faith development.

When I was around five years old, I sat in a Sunday School class and the dear woman who taught us was using a flannel board. She placed pictures of Abraham with a knife about to slay his son on the board. She said that he had great faith. Even at this young age I questioned how anyone could make such a statement.

I can still say that I learned all I needed to know from my parents and in our church of uneducated laborers. I learned that Jesus loved me. I learned that Jesus loves all people everywhere.

# Contents

*Preface* | xi
*The Gospel* | xv

## CATEGORY I: REVELATION, RELIGION, AND INTELLIGENCE

### Christian Revelation | 3
   Revelation and the Suffering Servant | 6
   Goads | 9
   Abraham the First Monotheist | 11

### Christianity Is | 13

### Christianity Is Not Impotent | 20
   God Wins | 20
   Reconciling the OT with Jesus | 23
   Correcting Theology | 24
   Sacredness | 25
   Christianity: the Power to Change the World | 26

### Religion Is | 28
   The Religious Teacher | 30

### Intelligent Spirituality | 32
   Education and Life Experience | 33
   An Example | 34
   The Spiritually Intelligent | 35

## CATEGORY II: PERENNIAL IDOLS

### Perennial Idols | 39
   Inevitability and the Reign of God | 41

### The Consuming Idol of Militarism | 42
   Cherubs and a Flaming Sword at Eden's Entrance | 48

Economics in Theological Thought | 50
   Introduction | 50
   A Summary on Scriptural Teaching for Just Economics | 51
   The Economics of Moses | 52
   The Prophets and God's View on Excess | 54
   Jesus' Philosophical Theology on Money | 55
   A Monetized World | 56
   Born in Debt | 59

The Banality of Evil and the End of a Nation | 61
   God wants a People, not a Nation-State | 65

The End of Idolatry | 67

## CATEGORY III: REALITY

Reality Creation | 75

The Underlying Structures of Reality | 80
   Sexuality and Structures of Reality | 84

Spheres of Existence and Human Reality | 87
   The Aesthetic Personality | 89
   Love and Comfort in Relation to the Aesthetic | 90
   The Aesthete and Social Cohesion | 91
   The Aesthetic Culture | 92
   Idolatry of the Human | 94

Chaos and the Human Condition | 96
   On Monsters | 97
   Naming Leviathan's Children | 98
   Living with Monsters | 99
   International Monsters | 101

## CATEGORY IV: SEX AND ROMANTIC LOVE

Sex, Violence, Sin, and Death | 105
   Sex and Sin Enter the World | 106

God's Heart for Sexually Exploited Persons | 109
   Scapegoating a Woman and Religious Violence | 110
   The Burden of Beauty | 111
   The Forgiven Escort of Faith | 113
   Endangered Guardians | 114

God, Romance, and Legacy | 117
    Romantic Love and Sexuality | 119
    Summary | 120
Repairing the World at the Root | 122
    The Lover's Dance | 122
    Learning to Listen | 125

## CATEGORY V: POPULAR MYTHS

Sexuality and the Metaphysical Myth of Modern Man | 129
    The End of Life | 130
The Myth of Race | 138
    Improper Words that Harm | 140
    Little Empires | 142
The Myth of Progress | 144
    Humanity has not Progressed | 146
    Becoming Human/Becoming Spirit | 146

## CATEGORY VI: BEING POOR/BEING HUMAN

The Sign of the Poor | 151
    The Earth is the Lord's | 153
    Literacy and the Poor | 155
    The Violence of Poverty | 156
Forever Human | 157

## CATEGORY VII: FORGIVENESS

Forgiving God | 163
God's Merciful Culpability | 170
    Forgiving God | 170

*Bibliography* | 175

# Preface

REFLECTIONS PRESENTS SEVEN CATEGORIES of thought, containing a total of twenty-five chapters. The chapters under each category consist of concepts and issues pertinent to today's Christian in America and abroad. The theology within the book's layout unfolds in an ordered manner, designed for Christian spiritual and intellectual formation in a world facing constant crisis. These categories of thought and the chapters under each were initially delivered as lectures to further the understanding of MTS (Master of Theological Studies) students on the importance of theological formation that nurtures thinking theologically about everything while seeking to bring healing to a broken world.

Part of the educational process is to be consistent while expanding upon previous instruction. This is accomplished through repetition. Repetition is useful for helping students retain the key conceptual statements of an idea or theological theme. The biblical writers used a form of repetition literary critics named *thematic progression;* this has been my practice in some instances. Thematic progression expands a true statement with further understanding. A conceptual statement or theological theme must demonstrate continuity across numerous subjects in order to be worth repeating. For these reasons, I have lines that are repeated across the seven categories.

The first category of thought is *Revelation, Religion, and Intelligence.* All three of these are dependent upon one another. Each one is foundational for the construction of a healthy and productive spiritual life. Understanding the concept of revelation is imperative for Christian faith, yet when reading or hearing the word most of the populace thinks of the biblical book rather than the religious concept.

True religion produces wise people who are peaceful and accepting of persons of other faiths. The acquisition of wisdom is congruent with intelligence. Because all religions are subject to emotion, the discipline of intelligent conversation is essential in a globalized world.

The second category is *Perennial Idols*. Under the naming of these idols I have written universal truths and identified specific instances in the present. I am indebted to Dennis T. Olson's book *The Death of Moses* for identifying these idols of death in Deuteronomy. The prophet Hosea also identified these three idols in a different manner. He offers the people a prayer of repentance that refuses the wealth of empire (Assyria), rejects military power (horses), and recants the idolatry of self-sufficient nationalism (work of our hands) rallied around false gods.

> *Assyria shall not save us;*
> *we will not ride upon horses;*
> *we will say no more, "Our God,"*
> *to the work of our hands.*
> *In you the orphan finds mercy.*
> (Hos 14:3)

The third category is *Reality*. I am simply fascinated as I think about God creating reality with all its variations in human experience. The reign of God is a reality introduced by John, taught by Jesus, and is awaiting our entrance in the now/not yet. In the meantime we all live in various interconnected temporal realities. It is my awareness of the reality of the poor that pulls at my thought all the time. Christianity is a reality-creating faith. We should all use language that aids and instructs us on how, within the values of Christian faith, to bring God into the world by conforming our thoughts and actions in concert with the will/reign of God.

My love for the portions and books of Scripture classified under the genre of wisdom literature has made me acutely aware of the voice of God in both the physical creation, and in the assorted relational realities we form as human beings. In particular is the indomitable reality of faith expressed through suffering.

The fourth category is *Sex and Romantic Love*. Sex is a problem for us human beings and this category contains brief reflections with some universal statements on sexuality. I hope these will be helpful to my reader. The chapter on God's heart for sexually exploited persons is meant to help us navigate beyond sexual ethics void of mercy and compassion.

I suppose I'm a romantic at heart. Romantic love is hopeful. It is consistent with the view of God for seeing the best in us. Faith exercises risk and romantic love is always subject to the risk of time. Romantic love hopes for a romantic response from the other. Romantic love is the playground of lovers; a place of sincerely held attraction which can mature to include kept promises. We all come to God out of need; we also need the dynamic of the male/female relationship in all of its potential for good. In the chapter on repairing the world at the root, I suggest that the overcoming of the disjunction in male/female relationships has the potential to fulfill all our efforts to heal the world.

The fifth category is *Popular Myths*. The word "myth" is used in this section to identify false ideological constructs. In particular, the myth of sexual identity as spiritual and not biological, the myth that moderns are more enlightened than people of the past, and the myth of race.

The sixth category, *Being Poor/Being Human,* is written to insist that the dignity, the humanity of the poor is superior to the righteousness of the rich. The chapter "Forever Human" establishes the permanence of the incarnation and reflects on what it means to be human.

The seventh category, *Forgiveness,* explores the culpability of God for reality and our need to forgive God, others, and ourselves. Although I affirm that God is guilty only of being merciful there are aspects of suffering that remain incomprehensible in relation to serving any imagined purpose.

# The Gospel

**GOOD NEWS IN A FEW WORDS.**

GOD WAS SO ENAMORED, so omnipotently in love with humanity that he joined the creation, irrevocably became a human being, made part of what it means to be God is to be human—allowed humanity to murder him and did so in a way that is revelatory of transcendent love and power—calling us all to recognize the sacredness of a human being. The only thing sacred to God is human life. This one fact, this reality, this truth, directs us toward a world without violence or greed; toward a Kingdom ruled by a revelation, by a man, by God, by a revelation that makes death (although painfully present) to be bereft of finality. Our unlimited imagination and all its powers are now directed toward being human in a way that fulfills the royal laws of loving God and neighbor (even our enemy) so that Christianity can be the most potent reality in a crooked world, a power that heals and straightens. Hope for the present is as important as hope for the resurrection! Like Jesus, we are to all be agents of change. "Thy Kingdom come . . .

# CATEGORY I

# Revelation, Religion, and Intelligence

# Christian Revelation

### Divine Touch

*Who are you?*
*Come I will show you*
*Just tell me*
*I cannot*
*Will you touch me?*
*I will*
*I am overcome*
*I see the invisible one*
*My being is changed*
*My consciousness invaded, heightened –*
*I will never be the same*

The Christian revelation is the product of God's self-revealing through the incarnation, life, teachings, death, and resurrection of Jesus. If God were to appear in his transcendence there would be nothing for humanity except a sense of the numinous. Transcendence brings us nothing and mystery is distraction from reality. It is the enfleshed entrance of God into the human family, as one of us, that provides us with a clear vision of who God is. We are called to follow his example.

The revelation of God in Jesus is superior to the revelation of God delivered to Abraham or at Sinai or experienced by the prophets. Yes, Christianity is the continuance of the work and revelation of God that began with Abraham. However, the faith we call Christianity is the apex of God's self-revelation. It is so complete as to be final; meaning all that can be learned of God has already been revealed in the stories of the gospel, the writings of the New Testament (NT), and in the *kerygma* (proclamation) of the word become flesh. There is no further revealing that can communicate the nature of God beyond the person of Jesus Christ, God's son.

Revelation, in this sense, is a purely religious concept that expresses the invisible deity's self-revealing. Human beings do not have an innate knowledge of God. We possess a moral conscience (which we can defy). We can view the external witness of creation (it is a display of power). We bear the image of God (which we mar with our freedom). The image of God in us is limited to the finer attributes of being human such as insight, love, compassion, to be relational, to act redemptively, to keep promises, and to participate in the creation of social reality.

God was able to become one of us because God related us to God's self when he created us in his image.[1] This being said, we can know God only if God reveals himself to us. To know God is not to describe God with terms that attempt to communicate God's otherness and omnific existence. We can come to know God because God reveals himself in order to be known. Knowing God is a relational matter that is accomplished through the conduit of faith upon hearing the narrative of God's self-revelation contained in Scripture.

Revelation questions all of reality. Revelation requires an abandonment of all contradictory theological concepts, and subjects all thought to the content of the revelation. For this reason the Christian revelation is authoritative over contradictory portrayals of God in the Old Testament (OT). The problem with these conflicting portrayals is in direct relation to how the writer perceives God in the world. One example is the expression

---

1. Jesus' self-appellation throughout the gospels is *son of man* and this title communicates his humanness. Jesus did not assert his deity but affirmed his experience as a human being without exception. The two natures argument is in opposition to the kenosis and challenges the omnific power and otherness of God to simply become a human being. It is clear that this dynamic of God living as a human being was not a masquerade, not a duality of being or *nature*, but a limiting of self so that the person of Jesus, the son of God, the word incarnate, the wisdom of God, could become the *son of man*. The mystery of the incarnation is a glorious revelation of God not subject to reason's finality. We human beings are all conscious recipients of life. God joined that life in all its finiteness and brought eternal life with him as he added humanness to his being. The incarnation was not a temporary state; God remains a man named Jesus. In this sense there has been a phenomenal change in the existence of God; it is at the essence of the gospel. This is so because it reveals God's great desire to join the creation in the only way he can: as a human being. We can say that God held back from God's self all that it meant to be God (except the image we bear) in order to become a human being. We cannot fully explain the being of God or the incarnation. We can receive his self-revelation.

of Jewish monotheism that can be referred to as *radical monotheism*. In this view, God is responsible for everything—even the failed choices of human freedom.

The portrayal of God in the Old Testament is subject to the consummate revelation of God in Christ found in the New Testament. This is a simple guideline for the Christian. When readings of the Old Testament conflict with the revelation of God in the New Testament the problem is not with God or even the text, it is with the interpreter's knowledge of Scripture and imagination—even the interpreter's revelation of God.

Literary criticism is essential for interpreting the OT in light of the NT revelation of God in Christ Jesus. For example, reading Joshua requires recognizing the genre of the book as a conquest narrative. Conquest narratives serve nation-states for co-opting the voice of God to justify the crimes against the former inhabitants of the land. The book of Joshua also contains literary hints that deconstruct the claims of God made in the book. The following piece from Joshua is one example:

> *Once when Joshua was by Jericho, he looked up and saw a man standing before him with a drawn sword in his hand. Joshua went to him and said to him, "Are you one of us, or one of our adversaries?" He replied, "Neither; but as commander of the army of the LORD I have now come." And Joshua fell on his face to the earth and worshiped, and he said to him, "What do you command your servant, my lord?" The commander of the army of the LORD said to Joshua, "Remove the sandals from your feet, for the place where you stand is holy." And Joshua did so.*
> Jos 5:13

When the angel of the Lord appears, he is not on the side of the forces of Israel or Jericho. Rather, he is present as a reminder of the revelation of God to Moses. This is depicted in the command for Joshua to remove his sandals because in the presence of God the ground is made safe. The angel of the LORD before Joshua is portrayed as the same God who met Moses at the burning bush. Moses, with God's help, delivered Israel from Egypt with a shepherd's staff. However the messenger holds a sword in his hand. Joshua is not like Moses, who provides God with a man whose sole defense from hostile forces is a walking stick. Joshua has chosen a sword. The imagery of the sword is reminiscent of the flaming sword at the entrance to the garden of Eden.[2] Humanity cannot enter the rest of God in his garden

---

2. The sword keeps humanity outside the garden, apart from the rest of God. Likewise,

sanctuary because humanity has learned to use fire and steel for warring. This piece in Joshua suggests that Joshua was given a choice to lay down his sword. God is portrayed as not being at war with humanity, neither with Israel or the people of Jericho. The theophany doesn't take sides; the sword is only symbolic in relation to Joshua.

The book of Joshua includes giants as a threat and so clues the reader in on the mythical nature of conquest stories, where the crimes of the conquerors are ignored because the people of the land are depicted as inferior (a giant is an aberration). Interestingly, in the Jericho story, the person with the most faith and education about the LORD and about the activities of Israel is a harlot. When the walls of Jericho fell, her home in the wall did not fall. So the walls of Jericho did not all fall down. The people were not all destroyed.

I have offered this brief view for reading Joshua to emphasize the subjecting of the OT revelation to the consummate revelation of God found in Jesus Christ the Lord. For those who are attentive to the theology and literary instruction of the text, the nonviolent God revealed in Jesus is present in the Old Testament.

The importance of the concept of revelation is essential for claiming that God reveals God's self over against ideas that insist God is the progressive creation of human need. Without the concept of revelation, religion is human invention. That the concept of revelation is not a part of the basic instruction for seminarians involved in critical thinking and being exposed to the realties that formed Scripture and history is tragic. This one failure results in the poverty of soul that results in atheism.

## REVELATION AND THE SUFFERING SERVANT

## Conviction

*Conviction born of an encounter with God is a word for expressing a change brought on by a phenomenal divine touch that enters into a human being, a change that gives witness to a power able to make any person who is recipient of such an encounter into an extraordinary soul. Such a person overcomes the world from within*

---

the sword in the hand of the LORD, who is standing before Joshua, signals the inevitable failure of Israel to enter God's rest—because they cannot be stopped from practicing war.

*and faces it outwardly with immovable courage and indomitable faith,
faith that is always motivated by love.*

The life of Paul portrays an uncommon power to live out a calling in the face of rejection and suffering. Paul lives without exhibiting uncertainty or doubt. In this sense Paul models a trait seen in Jesus. This trait is either unseen in the disciples or none of them lived it with the tenacity of this immovable convert named Paul, the violent, power-seeking, religious zealot who was called to be an apostle.

I think it is helpful to view Paul as more than a disciple, even as Jesus' replacement.[3] First, Paul's Damascus revelation is compatible with the call and commission narratives of the prophets. Yet, it is also distinctly more comparable with Moses' received revelations at the bush and at Sinai.[4] The formative preparation of Paul's life is noted in his educational studies. Beyond this, he becomes an example of grace. His conversion and life thereafter reflect the power of Christ Jesus to change a human life. If the murdering, religiously political zealot Paul can change, then anyone can. Paul viewed the grace given to him to be a pivotal moment in history (1 Cor 9:17).

## The Suffering Servant and the Apostle Called to Suffer

*Listen to me, O coastlands,
pay attention, you peoples from far away!
The LORD called me before I was born,
while I was in my mother's womb he named me.
He made my mouth like a sharp sword,
in the shadow of his hand he hid me;
he made me a polished arrow,
in his quiver he hid me away.*

---

3. Paul's self-understanding is consistent with this thought for Paul is more than one of the disciples. In his own thought he is an eschatological figure, a light to the gentiles. Paul appropriates Isaiah 49:6 to be expressive of his person and ministry (Acts 13:47).

4. Moses and Paul were both educated and guilty of murder. They both ask the heavenly messenger for his name. It is absurd to think that the purposeful theological structuring of Luke's second work would place so-called conflicting accounts of Paul's Damascus revelation by accident. The meaning behind each account, set alongside the other, offers the reader an opportunity to reflect on the understanding given to Paul that set his soul on a new course. It is apparent those with him gained neither understanding, nor revelation. Further, to think all that was spoken to Saul need be reported in any lived event is simply unrealistic. Luke's writing expects such awareness from literate persons.

# REVELATION, RELIGION, AND INTELLIGENCE

*And he said to me, "You are my servant,*
*Israel, in whom I will be glorified."*
*But I said, "I have labored in vain,*
*I have spent my strength for nothing and vanity;*
*yet surely my cause is with the LORD,*
*and my reward with my God."*
*Isa 49:1–4*

The suffering servant songs of Isaiah become particularly reflective of Jesus' experience and represent the Spirit of Christ. The perceived messianic aspect of the suffering servant songs is recognized in Jesus. Jesus ultimately becomes Israel by fulfilling the law and living out Israel's call. This being said, Jesus' experience with the disciples is continually marked by their failure to understand his words. The culminating moment is when they all scatter, marked off by Peter's denial. Even after the resurrection *some doubt.* Their ambitions overwhelm them and they remain in Jerusalem after receiving the Spirit; contrary to Jesus' words at his ascension. It appears that Jesus has labored in vain and spent his strength for nothing and vanity in relation to the disciples.

Jesus' appearance and calling of Paul is an act of God's constant freedom to work outside expected boundaries. The disciples, now apostles, have, if you will, competitors who are outsiders of their circle. The first is James. The appearance of Jesus to his brother James provides the disciples with a sensible leader. The martyrdom of Stephen sits in contrast to the disciples hiding during the time of Jesus' suffering. Then along comes this enemy, this religious zealot, who claims an encounter with the resurrected Lord, an encounter of a revelatory nature that challenges the secured place and role of the disciples:

*For I want you to know, brothers and sisters, that the gospel that*
*was proclaimed by me is not of human origin; for I did not receive*
*it from a human source, nor was I taught it, but I received it*
*through a revelation of Jesus Christ.*
*Gal 1:11*

God works slowly in relation to our expectations; ultimately Paul's formation occurs after his encounter with the Lord on the road to Damascus. In Arabia, Paul's sudden revelation is melded into his intellect, into his being; he worked out his theology during this three-year period in the company of the Spirit.[5] Paul has little need for the disciples and considers

---

5. At the interrogation of Paul by Festus, Paul is interrupted during his theological/

his calling to be of an eschatalogical nature (Acts 13:47). Paul disallows any need to even confer with the disciples whom he speaks of as being apostles before him. Paul is a man with a revelation.

## GOADS

> *When we had all fallen to the ground,*
> *I heard a voice saying to me in the Hebrew language,*
> *'Saul, Saul, why are you persecuting me? It hurts you to kick against the goads."*
> Acts 26:14

Our first picture of Saul is one of a powerful religious zealot in agreement with the killing of an alleged blasphemer. Saul launches out after the martyrdom of Stephen to become a sanctioned defender of God's ways by killing the blasphemy resident in an emerging sect of Judaism built upon faith in a leader who was also condemned for blasphemy.

When the Lord appears to Saul it is not a cordial event, as with Moses, who is drawn out of curiosity and invited to remove his shoes. Rather, like Abraham over Isaac with the knife, the Lord calls out Saul's name twice. The difference between the two men is profound at this point. Abraham is, by example, the father of faith, a uniqueness that attests to his status as a monotheist. Saul is not being tested, he is in conflict with the interests and salvific work of God.

The metaphor of kicking against the goads is instructive. Saul is like a harnessed animal, ignorant and stubborn. Saul ignores the structures of life and he cannot win against the greater power of the Lord. Saul has ignored the voice of God in creation, in the underlying structures of reality; he is outside the role of wisdom. Saul is guilty of not discerning the voice of the one in whom he believes: God. Within the metaphor is the interrogative *why* and this becomes an invitation to stop resisting. It also requires Paul to find God in the people and events that have occupied his efforts to persecute the persons involved in this emerging sect built around the person of Jesus.

---

historical defense and Festus claims that Paul's learning is driving him insane. This statement reveals the passion and intellect of Paul; he has no place for doubt. Festus's only defense against Paul's argument is to appeal to the fact resident in all religious belief, which is that in spite of a perfectly reasoned argument, the faith component suspends proof and holds it captive; Festus lacks faith.

Saul had been present at the stoning of Stephen, for he heard Stephen's sermon.[6] He had heard Stephen's prayer for God to forgive his murderers. In Stephen, Saul saw Jesus. I can think of no more profound preparatory event for Saul's revelatory encounter with Jesus, than for Saul to hear this Greek man proclaim Israel's history fulfilled in Jesus and then display to the world a grace (Stephen prayed for the forgiveness of those who were murdering him) that defied the suffering of death, even death by stoning. Stephen prepared Paul to receive his revelation. Stephen's conviction would live again in Paul. It was witnessing the death-defying conviction of Stephen that Saul kicked against that is recorded for all who read his story.

A revelation is an event. It occurs when a person is given in their soul an understanding about reality that is not learned but gifted. Yet, the ability to integrate a revelation into the life and intellect of a human being is dependent upon the human being. Even as we bring ourselves to the text as readers, we also arrive at a revelation event in all our limits as creatures. Saul's education and experience are essential to the reception of the revelation given to him. He was chosen. Further, it is fitting that the grace of God to redeem be exhibited in the man who becomes Jesus' replacement, and who will, in time, be considered as the founder of Christianity because of his role in the early missional works and writings of the burgeoning Christian movement. The role of Paul in the canon of the NT also attests to his importance as an eschatalogical figure. Only one thing can explain Paul, and that is his Damascus road experience. He met the risen Lord.

To claim a revelation can only be confirmed by living a life that affirms said claim. Paul's conviction is firm and immovable. He encountered the divine beyond the parameters of our known reality. It is so that Paul *despaired of life* at one point, not with doubt about the resurrected Lord, but over survival. Paul is often referred to as an obstinate personality and it is easy to affirm such a statement. The profundity of being a person with a revelation and charged with a task would make anyone seem obstinate. Perhaps only Abraham, Moses, and Paul display the life and actions of a person with a revelation. Jeremiah might be a candidate, but it is more likely that his theological imagination is more responsible for the profundity of his writings than a revelation.

---

6. Whether the sermon is an accurate account is irrelevant to the theological reading of Scripture. Scripture was written and inspired for the purpose of establishing theological instruction. Luke is more than a historian and his mind more complex than mere reporting.

Jesus, of course, displays a life built upon a revelation. Even though the formation of Jesus' self-identity can be studied, it is apparent he was the recipient of a revelation at an unidentifiable or particular moment. Jesus' personal growth to recognize himself as the suffering servant of Isaiah's songs, as the Israel God longed for embodied in a human being, sets Jesus apart from Abraham, Moses, and Paul. Although I believe that in Jesus God became a human being without exception, it is correct to say that the life of Jesus was watched over by God in a way that enabled Jesus, in his task, to reveal God in his flesh as a human being.

## ABRAHAM THE FIRST MONOTHEIST

### Confirming a Revelation

The importance of the concept of revelation is essential for claiming that God reveals God's self over against ideas that insist God is the progressive creation of human need. Without the concept of revelation, religion is human invention. Briefly, the revelation of monotheism given to Abraham is an interruption in human history. Monotheism is not part of an evolutionary cycle of humanity's evolving religious thought that ends in atheism (e.g., polytheism, pantheism, panentheism, monotheism, deism, agnosticism).

The monotheism of Abraham is established through his story in a variety of ways. Abraham's call acknowledges the God who speaks to him is not confined to a particular land or people. Further the God of Abraham will create his own people through an old man whose wife is beyond the years of childbearing. That Abraham's God is without a people is instructive for understanding that Abraham's God is unknown to humanity. Further, Abraham's God is not limited by human capability to reproduce nor is God subject to time. Meaning God is the creator of life and not subject to the powers of death. For this reason God can make promises that reach beyond the life of Abraham and into the drama of human history.

Abraham is a model of *conviction*. He never doubts the existence of this God who speaks to him. He does ask for personal certainty concerning God's promise that he would have an heir. The covenant ceremony in Genesis 15 through the act of splitting animals in half and placing them in a *wadi* as God symbolically (a smoking pot and flaming torch) passes down the center of their carcasses indicates that God is incapable of breeching a promise.

The ceremony suggests that to break the covenant is to suffer the same fate as the sacrifices. God would rather cease to be than violate his *sworn* promise to Abraham.

Not that God could be dismembered or cease to exist, but the ceremony exposes the heart or *holiness* of God. Abraham's God is of a nature contrary to all of ancient humanity's perceptions of their gods.

In light of these thoughts on Abraham and monotheism, understanding the *Aqedah* (the binding) in a manner consistent with the writer of Hebrews and the thought of Kierkegaard is, in my thinking, imperative.[7] Abraham's God is not like any other, this Abraham knows, for he is the recipient of a revelation that produced his life as a model for monotheistic faith.

The *Aqedah* is an unmatched test worthy of, and solely for, the father of faith, the one to be the recipient of the revelation of monotheism. It functions as a test only if Abraham believes in a good God who has promised him seed through Isaac, a God who alone is God over life and for whom the power of death is voided.

Abraham is not beginning his faith journey in Genesis 22. Rather, it is the culmination of his faith story. Afterward, Sarah dies and Abraham simply fades into history a happy sheikh whose wealth and power provides him with the company of beautiful women and lots of children.[8]

I am convinced it is correct to say when the LORD spoke to Abram in Genesis 12:1–3 he received a revelation of God that is demonstrated throughout his life to be monotheistic belief.

---

7. The writer of Hebrews understood that Abraham's belief in God's power to keep his promise in spite of the death of Isaac represented the necessity of resurrection. In effect, God and Abraham are in a contest where Abraham's faith matches God's power. However, the sacrifice of Isaac was never God's intent. The *Aqedah* should be called the *Nasa*, meaning the test. In this sense, the testing of Abraham is a polemic against child sacrifice. Kierkegaard explains Abraham's actions as a relational reality in which there is a teleological suspension of the ethical.

8. Abraham is also a man of his times and it was a time when men took multiple women for child-bearing. Sarah was known for her beauty; Abraham also loved Sarah and did not seek other women for child-bearing. It was Sarah who prompted Abraham to take Hagar. In this sense, Abraham was a model for monogamous marriage. His later years represent the goodness of God to extend his life with blessing. Abraham continued to live and breathe in an imperfect world where death reigned. Luke addresses the times past when God *winked* at humanity's models for living that were less than God's intent.

# Christianity Is

### Jesus Is Christianity

*Son of*
*God become human without exception*
*Exemplar*
*nonviolent resistor of systemic evil*
*love embodied*
*revealing God—suffering death,*
*not fighting back—loving us to death*
*Author and Finisher*
*arms outstretched, forgiving, embracing, hanging on a cross*
*Follow me*

CHRISTIANITY IS OFTEN IDENTIFIED as the doctrinal claims of institutions that benefit those who govern through adherence to their particular set of dogma. In this situation, what we need is clarity on those enduring realities that constitute Christian faith. This is so because Christianity, in all its glory as light and salt in a world of darkness, has been lost, misrepresented, and politicized, and in effect what exists is spiritually impotent.

### What Is Christianity?

*Christianity is a breach upon the world's sociopolitical order. It is the beginning of the end of reality as constructed by humanity—a reality inconsistent with God's will. Christianity's breach into the sphere of human existence is a challenge for humanity to reimagine the world with God. Christianity is a radical message of freedom, in which humanity chooses to follow the teachings of Jesus without restraint; without excusive reasoning that justifies the concept of the secular. Christianity demands the immediate sacralizing of every human being's life. Human beings alone hold the position of being sacred before God. Christianity accepts the nonviolent teaching of Jesus as essential practice for expanding the breach of God's entrance into the world. Christianity is the singular power potent enough to change, to save, the world.*

Jesus' ministry began with John's announcement of the impending arrival of a kingdom whose origin was from beyond, from God. In this sense the reign of God in Christ does not find its origins in David, and its entrance is indicative of the beginning of a new reality, a reality recognized by the prophets in their hope pieces. The prophets envisioned a world where every person knows the Lord and war is abolished, a world where even nature is arrested and transformed.

This breach of reality requires that all humanity has known or experienced in the past be understood as being less than God desires; it must come to an end. God's desire is that every human being would know his voice, hear it, and willingly live in accordance with his will. God wants to be known. God can be known, but his existence cannot be proven. The hope of existence is God. Reality's hope for eternity is the end of death. Jesus' life is the existence of God in the face of death's seeming finality. The breach is established and held in place by the unending life of Jesus. Transcendence offers nothing; it is because God joined the creation that we can become recipients of resurrection, of eternal life.

All of creation is a product of God's imagination. However, social reality is a construct formed through human relationships. To practice suffering love, forgiveness, and mercy, and to reimagine this reality is the practice of Christianity. It is our call to become children of God. To reimagine reality is a Christian practice, a spiritual practice. It is to align us with the will of God for humanity. It brings God into the world. Reimagining reality is to question the permanence of institutional inevitability as the governing power over humanity.

*Christianity is socially egalitarian by nature. This is so because love and the sacredness of every human life comprise the ultimate concern of God. Christianity is a reality-consuming faith because it is the unseen God made present in flesh and ultimately in all humanity. Christianity is the ongoing salvation of God's redeeming work in creation and for humanity.*

# CHRISTIANITY IS

*Christianity is always more than and greater than any institution attempting to identify itself with or as Christianity.*

Christianity is the freedom to live in the yes to God. The present state of humanity is life in both the yes and the no directed at God, that is, good and evil. Christianity is to follow and live out the life and teachings of Jesus. The no, the secular, is the refusal, it is the lack of courage to live in faith and follow Jesus through a narrow, one-person-wide gate.

*Christianity is a power that produces exemplary people whose lives are marked by a profound sense of humility and personal suffering over the condition of the world. Christianity is relentless in the proclamation of good news: built around the particularity of Jesus Christ as the coming of God, as the apex of God's self-revelation, as a spiritual movement of subversive power that is set to liberate humanity from all that does not represent God.*

Christianity is merciful, yet ever calling her members through the gauntlet of repentance where change of one's very being occurs. Because sin, as we know, is common to the human experience, repentance is a painful but healing gift. Repentance is completed when guilt is replaced with the restful touch of God, even though the consequences of our sin remain in the world.

Christianity is revelatory, for it is God who calls and works in those who receive the *kerygma* (proclamation). God has joined the creation and made part of what it means to be God is to be human. This act of love, God's longing to join the creature in the adventure of creative reality, is indicative of the sacredness of every human being. Life has meaning because God cares, God watches, and God is one of us. The kingdom of heaven is our salvation made present in a world that is not the way it is supposed to be. Christianity is a lived practice and the living is more important than petty dogmas.

*Christianity is to connect with the pathos of God.*

Because God is love, the pathos of God for the suffering of humanity is ever immediate and always intense. This being said, a person experiencing the pathos of God weeps and desires to alleviate suffering caused by injustice, catastrophe, and war. Where Christianity is, there are tears over the evils of human suffering, particularly that which is caused by human action. The pathos of God also moves those so touched to action. Where Christianity is, there are people helping the suffering.

*Christianity is a struggle.*

The kingdom of God is now/not yet, it is yet to swallow up the present but it has begun. The now/not yet transformative infusion of the reign of God into reality allows for two overlapping and incompatible realities to exist simultaneously. The yeast in the meal ultimately cannot be resisted, but in the present, Christianity lives within a state of struggle. Life is permeated with death. Good is present, but sin corrupts. Human beings who follow Christ struggle to live and produce life, while death still reigns and sin still corrupts. Christianity is a struggle to expand the breach that is the Spirit of Christ in humanity working to overcome the world.

*Christianity is by nature incompatible with the state.*

The appointing of a king, a president, or any head of a nation-state, of necessity must include a hierarchal system of those persons who will implement his/her will and decrees. It is true to say that human beings are not fit to rule over one another. Further it is true to say that God did not create us to rule over one another. God desires a people, not a nation-state.

*Christianity is constantly involved in education for the spiritual, physical, and intellectual betterment of humanity.*

It is the divine will's word that we are to "love one another." This being so, Christians understand that the development of every human being is an imperative. The development of the mind is to be congruent with the transformative work of the Spirit. To be drawn into the life of Christ in the present is an invitation to contemplative thought over the human condition and the reconciliatory work of God. Learning to think critically is learning to know how to "answer every one" (Col 4:6). To think theologically about everything is a spiritual discipline for the mind that enables physical flourishing for humanity.

To be Christian is to learn all one is enabled or blessed to, in any field of study or craft, so that this learning might be given to others. Christianity opens the heart and mind to unquenchable curiosity over all that can be learned under the sun. A curious mind is a healthy soul.

# CHRISTIANITY IS

*Christianity is present when the poor are educated and lifted into the social economy as flourishing members.*

It is un-Christian to withhold knowledge from others for the sake of economic gain. God does not leave his children foolish. Where Christianity is present, then education for all is also present. Although a person may specialize in a given field of study, in a Christian community knowledge is shared freely.

*Christianity is present when peace is sought without recourse to violence.*

Jesus was a man of peace and taught that the qualifying evidence of a child of God is to be a peacemaker. Christianity and violence are incompatible. Jesus' life and teaching exemplify nonviolence. Jesus' refusal to resist his murder upon a cross reveals to us the heart of man and the heart of God. The cross (God's participation in the cross of love) says God will not kill us, but will let us murder God in the world, and we do so every day that we reject God's voice; it is to say no to the good. Jesus taught that we are to resist evil with good and to love our enemies.

*Christianity in the present is subject to eruptions of both chance and evil where the absurd absolves the world of meaning; where meaning exists only in hope, through faith, knowing that God is watching—that God cares.*

The absence of God is theologically instructive, a literary motif throughout Scripture, and a daily experience. Yet, Christianity fails to instruct her adherents in the church to affirm this truth. In the church, everything becomes providence and is given an explanation. This explanatory effort is as absurd as the unexplainable, meaningless evil that permeates life and reality.

In Christianity the word "tragedy" is seldom used. When it is, it is swallowed up in the ensuing trust that God has somehow blessed the victim with needed lessons for their life, or the victim of the tragic becomes an exemplar of faith for their refusal to acknowledge God's absence in the tragic.

The absurdity of evil is often seen in tragic events that were products of chance. These calamitous moments disrupt life without warning. This disruption devalues existence; it rips at the fabric of hope and captures its victims in the grips of its permanence. A happy theology is simple-minded coping that ignores reality. Yes, the Lord brings us joy—in the midst of our sufferings.

The brevity of life is matched by the fragility of life. Both mark the human condition as subject to suffering and death. Christianity's power lies in a judgment that affirms God is watching and in a hope that meets eternity in the face of Jesus. A life of self-aggrandizement is a life in rebellion to the lessons of absurdity, the tragic, and evil and death, which are the foils for our faith.

How we respond to the suffering in the world is the evidence of knowing Christ. If we are governed by our ego, we cannot be responsive to the voice of God in a world marked by suffering. Humility in concert with a passion for merciful justice and how to live out truth is the mark of a Christian life.

*Christianity is present when prisons are closed and prisoners redeemed.*

Moses' life in Egypt provided him with the knowledge of how political powers jail and treat those they render unfit to live with society. So, Moses does not institute a penal system of incarceration, but rather he provides cities of refuge where the guilty (particularly anyone who has caused the death of another) can live together with their families (Num 35). Christianity is not supportive of a criminal justice system without restoration and opportunity for restitution over crimes committed. The for-profit prison system in the US is a sign of the economic stratification of society in a way that allows for unlimited wealth appropriation to flourish. This single flaw in our systems of law is more threatening to life than all the prisoners we have locked away.

*Christianity is present when war is understood to be an intolerable madness not to be taught to our children.*

When I went through the plague narratives of Exodus to uncover the acts of mercy that hardened Pharaoh's heart, I came across one event that simply defied all reasonable response.[1] It was the madness of Pharaoh to pursue the Hebrews into the sea. Pharaoh had been left his chariots as a

---

1. See Garner, *Interpretive Adventures*, 54–63. It is my position that Pharaoh's heart was hardened by God's acts of mercy during the plagues. Each plague is communicative and contains God's revelation of self amidst the liberating acts of power. It must be said that the plague narratives are also revelatory about human behavior, particularly that of a demagogue.

deterrent to Egypt's enemies after the liberation of the slaves. The author of the text is careful to include this bit of information, the preservation of the chariots, and its meaning includes the response of Pharaoh to God's mercy—Pharaoh is at war with God. After all the power of God exhibited in the plagues, Pharaoh's response, his pursuit of the Hebrews into the sea is madness. War is madness. War is an act against both God and humanity.

Christianity is the refusal to teach war as a legitimate response to the problems of shifting powers over humanity. Christianity exists and cannot be contained. It is God's work. All human efforts to limit or control the in-breaking reality of salvation, of heaven, of the Spirit, are chaff. God wins.

# Christianity Is Not Impotent

**GOD WINS**

*Sweet Breaking*
*The entrance of God*
*Enfleshed in people*
*Possibility ready to be imagined*
*Bending the will of the world*
*Wisdom and nonviolence prevail*
*God's will accomplished*
*The world will dance*

*nevertheless—as I live, and as all the earth shall be filled with the glory of the LORD. . . Num 14:21*

This elliptical phrase from the book of Numbers leaves the LORD's thought unfinished. We receive only an oath, an irrevocable proclamation and promise. The oath expresses the desire of God for all humanity to hear his voice, to see the land healed because humanity lives out, and lives in the glory of the LORD as his children. Yet how all this will happen is not said, it is to be imagined, then lived, as we all grow in the knowledge of the Lord Jesus Christ.

WE CAN KNOW GOD but we cannot prove God exists. However, we can remove any negating assertion in a similar statement. I know Christianity is not impotent and it can be proven theologically in the realm of intellect, existentially in the lives of martyrs and exemplary souls, and practically in the world. The hope pieces of Scripture express the hope of God for humanity. God's hope is not vain. The eternal triad of faith, hope, and love bring the presence of God into the world and actively work toward a redemptive reality both now and yet to come.

Often people will state portions of Scripture without even knowing what is meant or being able to answer with any viable articulation. For instance, "We are all children of God because we are created in his image." However if asked to define with clarity the image of God borne by humanity, they struggle to respond. The image of God in humanity is easily seen in the study of God's activity in redemptive history. God is a relational, redeeming creator who keeps his covenants. We too are relational, we are drawn to redemptive stories, we participate in the creation of reality, and we make promises; these, along with insight and the capacity to love, are definitive aspects of the image we bear. Within the immediate setting of Genesis 1:26, it is apparent that humanity is the apex of God's creatures, and is able to subdue creation because of likeness and image.

Something is missing, however; it is a clear definition on the "likeness." Scripture states that we are created in both the likeness and image of God. Understanding likeness is crucial for speaking theologically about the human condition. It is important to note that Genesis 3:2 is an ellipsis. It communicates that God is troubled by announcing an alternative for humanity other than eternal life:

> *Then the LORD God said,*
> *"See, the man has become like one of us, knowing good and evil;*
> *and now, he might reach out his hand and take also from the tree*
> *of life,*
> *and eat, and live forever. . ."*

As the creation narratives unfold it is apparent that likeness finds its consummation after eating the prohibited fruit.[1] The power of choice, the freedom to reach beyond the structures of reality, even to say *no* to God, belongs to humanity. However, because humanity is self-destructive, impatient, and chooses to kick against the goads, life without end has become out of reach. God has given us freedom both to say *no* to God (not a wise move) and to create our own reality. It is the violation of our freedom that exhibits likeness, because we experience knowing evil. God knew about evil, and in creation, God, in his grace, allowed for evil to exist. Evil is initially foreign

---

1. Although the Hebrew noun "likeness" is not used in Genesis 3:22, the preposition is still compatible with the intent and meaning of "like" or "as."

to God.² For us, evil brings death and is multiplied in our many sins. Our freedom as creatures in the likeness and image of God is so honored by God that he never violates our will.³ Since a sane person has never said, "I've solved the problem of evil" I will leave this quandary knowing we are limited and as Qohelet says,

> ... then I saw all the work of God, that no one can find out what is happening under the sun. (Eccl 8:17)

God never wins through coercive force. Existence is real, not written; God wins by revealing God's self to be love and goodness. We err when we think humanity is not responsible for the reality we have created. The story of Jesus is an event that exposes the cycles of violence that permeate human history. Through the revelation of God crucified, the Spirit of the Lord enables us to imagine humanity's rejection of violence. This is accomplished through the reign of God, through being in Christ, by entering the rest of God, by living with eternal life as a conviction that cannot be conquered. In Christ we are empowered as recipients of the Spirit to change history. Christianity is not impotent. God is love, not a warrior or a monster.

Christianity is a religion to be practiced, and a way of life to be learned. It was systematically dismembered by being assimilated into the powers of human government through elitist structures of power. It was reduced to dogmatism, and claims of correct belief became the idols that required the death of any resistor. Correct belief became more important than living a faith that requires love of neighbor as the evidence of love for God. God's mercy sees the heart, while *correct belief* resists maturation and negates insightful theology through useless pedagogic claims.

---

2. Initially, God experiences evil vicariously through his love for humanity. In Christ, God experiences evil without participating in it, yet God *knows* evil directly through experiential suffering of evil in the Lord Jesus.

3. Although God does not violate the human will, God does influence our will. The power of God to influence the will is a task to imagine in all its possibilities and complexities. However it does not appear within the experience of humanity that God actively influences human will for controlling our development or history. The exception is certainly those persons like Abraham, Moses, and Paul, who are given a revelation. The prophets were also beneficiaries of gracious influence. Outside of these exceptions it seems that God's influence is limited to the people who say *yes* to him, to those who hear and obey, and who, through likeness and image, through faith, bring God into the world.

## RECONCILING THE OT WITH JESUS

The misperception that the OT supports violence is an incorrect interpretive lens. The confusion for NT believers results in either a God in process or a dualistic God that is both violent and uncontrollably angry.[4] The OT read through the lens of Jesus as the consummate revelation of God along with the application of genre to OT books easily dismantles violent readings.

It is imperative to learn that every time the OT uses a Yahweh speech formula ("Thus says the LORD") the reader must consider the genre of the book, the speaker, and the view of God represented in the claim. A reader's misperception of the Yahweh speech formula as inviolable surrenders their own power to think critically about claims and actions inconsistent with the character of God. Further, all purposeful literary design that demonstrates great care and effort in producing Scripture is lost if the speech formula cannot be questioned.

Once a person learns to read the Christian canon in its entirety, free from the errant concept of God-sanctioned violence, then the message of Jesus becomes the kind of good news that makes redemption both personal and grounded in OT history without contradiction. To annul the gospel of Jesus and his message, a message meant to change the world, by accepting violence as normative and war as inevitable, is to reject the gospel and reduce it to impotence. It is because of accepting violence as normative and war as inevitable that Christianity is filled with a history of violence, war, and horrible crimes against humanity—often done in the name of Jesus.

Within the teaching of Jesus and the theology of Scripture are revelations on humanity that, coupled with the Spirit, are able to quite literally change the world. To abandon this thought is to lose faith, hope, and love to inevitability. It is unfortunate that Scripture is read in a manner that only seeks to interpret God. The Scripture is written to enable us to find God, and in doing so, we learn about ourselves. This is so because in the creaturely reality God must always be enfleshed, must speak, and must hear. This being said, Scripture is instructive on all that impedes humanity from being the people of God, and impedes Christianity from presenting the good news as historically salvific, not merely personal.

---

4. I think it is correct to consider human existence in Christ to be a learning experience for God. The nature of God (holiness) prohibits any sort of change in God that challenges the constancy of God's character as *the* moral being.

## CORRECTING THEOLOGY

I do not think that saying we are totally depraved is correct; it is a hopeless statement, bereft of faith, and void of love in its description of the human condition. Acceptance of our humanity is impossible when such extreme statements as "total depravity" govern our concept of human potential in Christ and in the emergence of the reign of God in the present:

> *When gentiles, who do not possess the law, do instinctively what the law requires, these, though not having the law, are a law to themselves.*
> *They show that what the law requires is written on their hearts, to which their own conscience also bears witness;*
> *and their conflicting thoughts will accuse or perhaps excuse them on the day when, according to my gospel, God, through Jesus Christ, will judge the secret thoughts of all.*
> *(Rom 2:14–16)*

When Paul speaks of people who live acceptable lives, according to their moral conscience, it is clear that total depravity is inconsistent with Paul's thought. The first murder, found in the story of Cain and Abel, demonstrates that Cain has the power of choice:

> *The LORD said to Cain, "Why are you angry, and why has your countenance fallen?*
> *If you do well, will you not be accepted? And if you do not do well, sin is lurking at the door; its desire is for you, but you must master it."*
> *(Gen 4:6–7)*

If our power to choose good is removed from us because of some primal event and those born afterward inherit this untenable condition, then God is at fault.[5] The general attitude produced by the ideology of hereditary sin abolishes hope before we even begin. The theology that follows spends its energy on justifying God and becomes esoteric in the sense that it is logically absurd and yet is defended by persons who are supposed to be

---

5. I think it is obvious to think of the human condition as subject to limitations because we are creatures. To think that redemption and resurrection are inevitable for our present state is instructive, and essential, for our present state was never considered to be permanent. Like Adam and Eve, we all fall; innocence is an unsustainable condition for humanity. Our fall is inevitable. Our ability to choose good is because we bear the image of God. We all experience the garden of life in innocence, as children, but the way is barred by our inherent limitations as creatures of flesh learning to be spirit.

both sane and wise. If our freedom to choose is abolished and we have lost *likeness*, then any relational reality between humanity and God is nullified.[6]

## SACREDNESS

In the life and teaching of Jesus it is clear that the preservation of life defines how the Torah is to be read; this is also so for a good reading of the OT. The only sacred object in the eyes of God is humanity, each one of us. For this reason we see all claims of sacredness attributed to symbols, ceremony, and location as ideas to be rejected, just as they were by the prophets. This truth is a basic tenet of Scripture and its ultimate declaration is quoted by Jesus, who raises the challenge to love of enemy; in effect, our enemy is our neighbor, who is to be loved.

> *You shall not take vengeance or bear a grudge against any of your people, but you shall love your neighbor as yourself: I am the LORD.*
> *(Lev 19:18)*

> *But love your enemies, do good, and lend, expecting nothing in return. Your reward will be great, and you will be children of the Most High; for he is kind to the ungrateful and the wicked.*
> *(Luke 6:35)*

The brother of Jesus, in the epistle bearing his name, turns all religious effort toward the weakest persons in society. James teaches that religion is corrupted when it does not serve the needy, this simple truth that the purpose of religion, that the worship of God, is accomplished when, like God, we love and honor humanity as sacred. For this reason the massive effort to accumulate weapons designed to be nothing more than massive explosions able to destroy both the ground and human life represents an immorality that is unconscionable. In the alleged civilized world of state power, life is not sacred, only the state, only their power. Our greatest threats are the very structures that we expect to bring order to life because these powers do not seek peace, but rather to dominate others and seek unjust gain. Laws that are void of sacredness bind them, so they regulate evil rather than do good.

The world needs a religion of peace, a religion free from the idols of militarism, materialism, and nationalism, a religion free from useless

---

6. Likeness is fulfilled in knowing both good and evil, but always choosing the good, which aligns us with the goodness, holiness, nature, and Spirit of God.

theology that contributes nothing to the healing of the world. The world needs Christianity to be wrestled away from ignorance, popular culture, the state, and therapeutic, feel-good reductionism. God entered the world in the person of Jesus and introduced to us a way of living that leads to the healing of the world.

## CHRISTIANITY: THE POWER TO CHANGE THE WORLD

Christians are to be creators of reality. The reality we create is first within; it is unconquerable because of the God who empowers us, and because we receive the Spirit of the Lord in our bodies. Our status as aliens is to be seen as a difference so profound that our lives are a mixture of radical goodness and a groundedness that focuses our love on people in the present. Although the world cannot see it, a mature Christian is a person so grounded in reality that they see through all of the world's guises and view God as waiting for our response to the present.

The interrelational reality created in Christian community is to be an affective embodiment of God. It is a place where a practical balance of separation from and engagement with the world is integrated into daily life. It is a place where people of all ages learn to find God in the world and, most importantly, to bring God into the world through their thoughts and practices. People need to be taught how to live in relation to one another. Social intelligence is for everyone. However, it is not mere civility or niceties, it is recognition of the other, it is to understand reality-creation as Christian practice. Social intelligence is not ignoring reality or classifying people as toxic, but rather it is born of spiritual intelligence. It is wisdom schooled in the classroom of love and insight.

*Blessed are the peacemakers, for they will be called children of God.*
*(Matt 5:9)*

Christians are peacemakers. Peacemaking requires courage and resistance to evil. Peace is always governed by love and mercy. Peacemaking always utilizes wisdom and nonviolence. In Jesus' statement from the Sermon on the Mount, the qualifying activity of a child of God is peacemaking. It is reasonable to say that warmongering is disqualifying to the position of living as one of God's children.

I think at this point in my reflection it is evident that the education of a person is not the systemic method present in schools across the US. Rather, education's emphasis on human development, maturation, and learning peace is the activity of a community and leads to a hunger for learning.

In conclusion to this piece, I must say that at the root of all violence is the failure of men and women to live together without domination. Herein lies the healing of the world, for us to learn to live together as gendered beings comfortable in our skin, housing the Spirit, ever serving one another for the flourishing of life.

# Religion Is

### Unafraid of Religion

*God of all people*
*Will you speak beyond the cloud?*
*Humanity's wilderness journey*
*Living without hearing*
*The ultimate pedagogy*
*Love God*
*Love others as yourself*
*Can we search together?*

RELIGION IS THE SEARCH for God because it seeks to provide meaning for life. Without religion life is meaningless. According to James (the Lord's brother), religion is an awareness that God is watching to see how we will live in a world of injustice, where evil exists alongside goodness. That God is watching is made clear by James, because religion is to be practiced "before God":

> *If any think they are religious,*
> *and do not bridle their tongues but deceive their hearts,*
> *their religion is worthless.*
> *Religion that is pure and undefiled before God the Father, is this:*
> *to care for orphans and widows in their distress,*
> *and to keep oneself unstained by the world.*
> *(Jas 1:26–27)*

The purpose of religion is, for most people, overlooked. The purpose of religion is to change the practitioner or believer into a person of self-control, peace, and love, into one who actively pursues the healing of the world through suffering-love. Anything else is inconsistent with the purpose of religion; it is an aberration. Learning to love, to be spiritual, is the heart of religious pursuit. Believing that God is watching and is pleased by this activity is good religion.

The perennial questions "Who am I?" and "Why am I here?" must necessarily be followed up with "How can I control my desire?" and "Is life about compliance with religious authority or about learning to love?" According to James, serving the weak and defenseless, serving those whose lives are touched daily by the presence of death, is religious practice. It is notable that James ignores all symbol and ceremony in his brief and rich statement on religion. For this reason, religion must first be inward, giving birth to a will that is at odds with the world.

The search for God is part of human experience. The Gospel of John's statement on the identity of God is universally above any other idea; God is love. John's statement rests upon the foundation of monotheism in which God is "one," a living Spirit (Deut 6:4). Luke recorded Paul's sermon to the Athenians and accredited the search for God by various people groups as God's purpose in the development of humanity (Acts 17:22–31). The search for God is to be honored when it is functioning within the constraints of good religion.

Christianity is based upon the concept of revelation. The consummate revelation of God is Jesus Christ, the word made flesh, the apex of God's self-revelation to humanity. The incarnation of God is not merely an idea brought about by natural progressive thinking about a deity. The incarnation is a revelation confirmed in the resurrection of Jesus and in the present through the faith experience of Christians who live out the purpose of religion.

Religion is an individual inward pursuit for the divine, because the inward need to understand reality and hope for or have faith in a living God is universal. Religion is a social reality subject to the incorporation of aesthetics and ethics. Further, the institutionalizing of religion requires religious authority, signs, symbols, and ceremonies to guide others toward James's concise statement of pure and undefiled practice. The goal of religion is spiritually mature human beings who express the divine as exemplars of the respective faith who live independent from the pedagogy of signs, symbols, ceremony, and the basics of their faith.

# REVELATION, RELIGION, AND INTELLIGENCE

## THE RELIGIOUS TEACHER

Religion is such an abused reality in relation to the thoughts and practices of human beings. Multitudes of people claim to know God and use religion in ways that cannot be reconciled with the purpose of religion. I am fond of saying, "Any religion that promotes violence is not worth the paper its Scripture is written on." It is amazing how many persons claiming Christianity ignore their own *religion* and think I'm talking about *other* religions.

Because of the way most Christians read the Bible they are unable to receive the nonviolent instruction in the violent stories of the OT. Stories of violence in the name of God are immediately suspect and subject to critique. These stories reflect more about humanity than they do God. The state and religious institutions always co-opt the name of God for their own purposes; this is so with every religion. The deification of the state and religious authority is a common form of idolatry. This idolatrous abuse is so common that it is recorded in the Decalogue under the prohibition for assigning the name of God to the vanity of human affairs:

> *You shall not make wrongful use of the name of the LORD your*
> *God, for the LORD will not acquit anyone who misuses his name.*
> *(Deut 5:11)*

James provides some advice that all religious people need to heed. First is to control your speech (1:26), and second is to avoid presumptuous knowledge that would lead a novice to thinking they are prepared to teach (3:1). The basic instruction of religious thought for mass consumption is essential pedagogy. However, a person who does not get beyond the mass presentation of religious thought is easily puffed up with limited knowledge and tends toward absolutist readings of Scripture.

The religious teacher's life is unlike the life of others simply because they are responsible for their pedagogy that should move those they teach to "pure and undefiled" religion. A religious teacher is a person who, like the prophets, has lived a life before God in which God has looked over their formation and guided their life. A teacher of religion has paid a price for their status as teacher; this is so for any religion. A teacher will be a voracious reader, is driven toward theological thought in all matters, and will be moved to write for the sake of others.

The writings of a religious teacher are not simple advice for feeling good about one's self, and they are not aesthetic works on achieving success. Rather, the writing of a religious teacher is an effort to bring God into the world through the application of theology to all of life. Writing is an expression of wisdom in every religion. Wisdom (beyond pedagogy) always wrestles with the responsibility of humanity before God and the absence of God in the world. These two, human responsibility and God's absence, are the playground of a good religious writer. Good religious writing that is consistent with the search for God always meets real-world issues with spiritual insight.

# Intelligent Spirituality

## The Thinking Christian

*Loving God with the mind*
*Contemplating God's greatest work*
*Image-bearing humanity*
*I will begin with myself—I am a human being*
*Searching for that image, that likeness*
*I am alive, a being—so is God*
*Theology is always ontological*

*You shall love the Lord your God with all your heart, and with all your soul, and with all your strength, and with all your mind; and your neighbor as yourself.*
*(Luke 10:27)*

FOR MANY IN THE world of Christianity the formation of a title with the words "intelligent" and "spirituality" would engender a distraction as though a misnomer was at play, or at least an oxymoron. This is an unfortunate perception because spirituality without the presence of intelligent thought is a fickle exercise in seduction, a self-deception, and voids any authorial dependency upon an intellectual approach to Scripture and life. This state of affairs allows unquestioned statements to pass for wisdom, and the erratic shaking of physical response to indicate spirituality.

*To truly be spiritually attuned to God is to embrace wisdom*

Intelligent spirituality is an awakening from death, from darkness, into life and light. Intelligent spirituality is the incorporation of the mystic and the intellectual into a flowing synthesis of knowing by knowing God and humanity, understanding reality, being adept at Scripture, and always exhibiting a desire to learn about everything. The person displaying intelligent spirituality longs for the constant application of theology to every aspect of life in the present and all of history. Intelligent spirituality is to face reality and bear the burden of reality as an agent of God's redemptive work in the earth.

Any spiritual practice that abandons intelligence for feeling, for communicating the transcendent through ceremony, is simply void of intelligence, because intelligence is meant to engage reality, the present moment, with the vigor of articulated truth. Transcendence brings us nothing; it is beyond us. Only the practical application of spiritual living that meets the physical reality offers us any change or benefit. Intelligent spirituality always seeks truth in all matters and is not subject to the ideological powers of symbols, ceremony, or state institutions. Intelligent spirituality is intricately produced from the study of Scripture for the sake of all humanity. It is expected that all God's children would grow in grace and the knowledge of Jesus. God does not desire that his (peacemaking) children remain ignorant.

## EDUCATION AND LIFE EXPERIENCE

God chose Moses, formed Moses' life, and called Moses. Moses was educated as an Egyptian, seasoned with age, and lived life within three different cultures—Egyptian, Hebrew, and Midianite. When Jesus' uneducated disciples were failing to understand the full impact of his life, he chose an educated Pharisee to live out the life that for Jesus had been cut short. Paul was an older man, a man of multiple cultures. He was a Jewish person who was educated like a Greek and yet was a citizen of Rome. Paul also depended upon the educated to read his letters publicly and teach those who were not privy to education. The finest of the prophets, like Jeremiah, were educated persons. To whom much is given, much is required.

# REVELATION, RELIGION, AND INTELLIGENCE

## AN EXAMPLE

I was speaking with a student from a local Christian university. He was majoring in social justice and studying environmental justice. When he shared this with me I laughed, smiled, and said, "Now that is a definite misnomer." I was simply amused at the simplification of a major theological theme—the healing of the earth—that flows throughout Scripture. Although pursuit of legislation to preserve the earth is an important activity, it loses its power to fulfill its goal if justice is not first and foremost a matter of care for humanity.

Justice is a relational word in Scripture. It is applicable to people. People can *do justice* and act with *mercy* as they walk humbly with God. The abuse of our environment is always a matter of failed justice in human affairs. You cannot provide healing or protection for the environment without the application of justice in human affairs. As long as injustice in society prevails, laws to protect the environment will also fail. The healing of the world begins with human flourishing, not the earth. A capitalist system is inevitably in conflict with responsible governing of humanity and therefore in conflict with environmental issues.

An intelligent spirituality in relation to the simple title "environmental justice" views the title as misleading and unhealthy for spiritual development. A more appropriate title would be "human flourishing and healing the Earth." These two are interrelated, inseparable, and you cannot address one without the other. However, the preeminence of justice for humanity is essential for environmental care. Shall we deliver justice to the environment? The Scripture clearly associates the connection of humanity's ethical and moral behavior with the ground. The failure in Eden left us to inherit a world with thorns and thistles. Hosea cries out that the shedding of blood is so common in the land that the land itself responds with a lack of life.

> *Therefore shall the land mourn, and every one that dwelleth therein shall languish, with the beasts of the field, and with the fowls of heaven; yea, the fishes of the sea also shall be taken away.*
> (Hos 4:3)

Not only do we destroy our living environment through acts of greed, it is God who has created the world in such a way that our moral behavior is reflected in the earth. Achieving justice is always first and foremost a matter of healing human relationships. Further, justice is set in poetic parallel lines with righteousness and the two are inseparable. The practice of the prophets is to also set the poor parallel with the word "righteousness." You cannot heal the environment without restoring the relationship that has been lost between the powerful and the powerless. This is a matter of justice. God is the healer of the land and this occurs only as humanity lives in merciful and just relationships with one another, especially in matters of land and economics.

## THE SPIRITUALLY INTELLIGENT

A spiritually intelligent person knows that the healing of the world begins with the healing of human relationships between culturally distinct groups, between the rich and the poor, and that healing is a matter of justice. Justice as a theological practice is not penal oriented but restorative. Justice in theological use is mindful of the systemic structures of evil present in all institutions. The surrender of the finer human attributes of love, compassion, mercy, redemption, reconciliation, and sharing to institutional rules is to lose our humanity.

Justice does not, in our world, work its way down from the top to the bottom, and God is not found in the halls of power. Rather, God is found where injustice has caused the most harm. The spiritually intelligent know that bringing human touch and a listening, compassionate ear to the poor is to experience the harmonious presence of God's love. It is a spiritual act to educate and empower the poor. It is a prophetic act to advocate on their behalf. Spiritual intelligence seeks to liberate the poor by creating an environment of sharing and communal flourishing.

A spiritually intelligent person is always compassionate and practices readings of Scripture from a lens of compassion rather than a legal lens. The compassionate lens is the most important position from which to read Scripture. Spiritual intelligence refuses the power held by the keepers of doctrine to interfere with the freedom of reading compassionately, morally, intelligently, and imaginatively. The prophetic imagination resists the keeper of the status quo.

A person maturing in spiritual intelligence experiences moments of deep intellectual catharsis. These revelatory moments overcome the mind with God's view on reality and provide clarity of vision. These times enable confidence in the reasoned speech of the recipient and are empowering to the soul. This spiritual experience is the product of learning to love God with one's mind through constant contemplative thinking, waiting, and searching. All of life is an opportunity to learn from God, and interpreting life in this manner leads to a spiritual intelligence born of an awareness that God is always watching, a consciousness of divine presence even when the absence of God is experienced. Intelligent spirituality refuses to release God from the forefront of all thought at all times. The spiritual intellect produces an indomitable faith.

# CATEGORY II

# Perennial Idols

# Perennial Idols

### I Don't Believe in Idols

*An idol is nothing*
*Ah, but it creates monsters when believed in*
*An idol can't speak*
*Ah, but its voice is the surrender of your freedom*
*Idols are for primitive people*
*Primitive people war, practice greed, their tribalism is your nationalism*
*I don't believe idols*
*Then believe God*

THE ENDURING IDOLS OF humanity that exist in every civilization are, overall, left unidentified and exist as normative parts of culture. These same idols pass over into religious thought and practice with the ease of a cool breeze. An idol is more than an image, it is an ideology. Perennial idols reach across time, across ethnic groups, and defy the borders of nation-states. They are constructs for living that are inconsistent with the desire and purposes of God. Perennial idols are a universal aspect of human life that consume goodness with the assertion that they are inevitable, essential, and normative parts of reality.

People surrender to these idols in part because they cannot imagine the world without them. These idols are the compromise of religious direction, goals, and function in churches without even an attempt to limit their dominance. Deuteronomy identifies these perennial idols as a continual temptation that exists after the primitive idols of images and polytheistic worship are defeated. Deuteronomy 6–11 provides commentary (teaching) on the Decalogue in chapter 5. The perennial idols are in opposition to the commandment to have no other gods before the Lord. These idols will survive the cleansing of the land and the ongoing effort to inhabit the land. They are identified in the following verses, not with a singular word, but with clarifying injunctions:

> *If you say to yourself,*
> *"These nations are more numerous than I; how can I dispossess them?"*
> *(Deut 7:17)*

The first injunction is set against the temptation to form society around the ideological trappings of depending upon a military force for safety and preservation of Israelite identity as the people of God. Although God would have used pestilence to drive out the inhabitants of the land, God cannot stop either the inhabitants of the land or Israel from warring. The identifiable idol that God seeks to end is a culture of militarism.[1]

> *Do not say to yourself,*
> *"My power and the might of my own hand have gotten me this wealth."*
> *(Deut 8:17)*

This injunction is set against the pride of self-sufficiency. Pride in self-sufficiency leads to the thought that wealth is solely a product of personal effort. This pride ignores God and the systems that produce wealth for a few. In such a setting, material gain becomes more important than moral development. It is the idol of materialism, of capitalism's unrestrained consumption, a system where people are divided into the rich and the poor.

> *When the LORD your God thrusts them out before you, do not say to yourself,*
> *"It is because of my righteousness that the LORD has brought me in to occupy this land"; it is rather because of the wickedness of these nations that the LORD is dispossessing them before you.*
> *(Deut 9:4)*

This injunction is a warning against the false pride of cultural superiority, of ethnocentrism, nationalism, and (supposed) moral correctness. Nationalist groups of people do not judge their actions in the world with sensitivity toward others. It is a people's history that reveals their view of

---

1. It is for this reason that the *ecclesia* should oppose the existence of a standing military. The *ecclesia* should teach their children to pursue peace and support nuclear disarmament.

self. When history is written by the conquerors it always justifies the actions of the conquerors and demonizes the conquered. The abuse of religion for supporting nationalism is at the heart of this injunction.

## INEVITABILITY AND THE REIGN OF GOD

Idols consume and confine human beings to a reality that claims legitimacy, but exists because of the rejection of God's voice and the subsequent mercy of God that allows us to live in spite of our erring choices.[2] Because these three perennial idols are universal to all peoples in all times and places, it is evident that they are a reflection of humanity's tendency to lose or misalign faith in God by deifying a temporary power.

The Christian claim is that God entered history by becoming a human being and that this act is decisive for the entrance of the reign of God over humanity. For this reason, inevitability, in relation to these universal perennial idols, is subject to the power of Christian faith. This being said, the presence of Christian faith in any given society is indicated by a push against and even an abolishing of these consuming idols. When Christianity as a religion becomes the keeper of inevitability and the voices for militarism, materialism, and ethnocentrism in society, then Christianity no longer exists.

Christianity is a humanizing power that liberates and provides the power for people to resist the cry of inevitability with an imagination that deconstructs the existing reality. The god of inevitability is a faithless heart, a heart held captive by fear. The Lord Jesus' vision for humanity is one of hope empowered by the Spirit. Hope defies inevitability and opens up all the latent imaginative power in freedom of choice when idolatry has sought to close the door. To surrender to inevitability is idolatry.

It is the reign of God that is inevitable and it has already begun in those who follow Jesus. Further, not only are believers called to resist the perennial idols, but to exist as persons completely free from their influence, people with a heart already in the world to come. To dream with God is to capture a vision for humanity that enters the present and heals the world.

---

2. Discerning the voice of God begins with recognizing the voice of God in creation, in our moral conscience, and in consistency with the image and likeness of God borne in our souls. Discerning the voice of God is an act of intelligence that begins with faith, and so is the perfect congruence of spirituality and intelligence that forms biblical wisdom.

# The Consuming Idol of Militarism

*Any religion that promotes violence is not worth the paper its Scriptures are written on.*

### The Consuming Fire

*The cult of the crowd*
*Lord Nuclear—god over all*
*War is a weapon of mass destruction*
*Line up now—offer your sons and daughters*
*Symbols and ceremony abound*
*Profiting from the business of war*
*The gods of the earth—giants of chaos*
*They all die*
*The main role of theology*
*Is application to human reality in the present moment.*

IN ORDER TO AFFECT a culture shaped by external forces of wealth and power, a culture of ideologies inconsistent with the growth and development of Jesus' vision for humanity, Christianity must establish cultural practices that promote critical thinking and replace the role of the external forces with alternative practices. Alternative practices are not accommodation; they continue to resist evil, and to support ethical and moral values consistent with Scripture and faith. The local church is intended to be a place where the reign of God is exhibited by all to see, it is to be an alternative community of practice that challenges all accepted norms that are inconsistent with loving God and one's neighbor.

Because alternative practices do not accommodate the dominant cultural and political powers, alternative communities are subject to suspicion and natural exclusion, whether by choice or by difference. The prophetic element of the alternative community is first demonstrated by their living out the reign of God in the present. Second is the practice of prophetic denunciation, that is, to speak against the idolatries of militarism, materialism, and nationalism.[1]

These perennial idols are not the idolatry of deifying the cosmos. Perennial idols enter the people of God as forces from outside the tenets of monotheism, of Christian faith. They belong to the ruling ideologies that enable human government, resist love of neighbor, and cannot celebrate difference. In the US, multiculturalism is the lie that supports assimilation, refuses to celebrate difference, and, via capitalism, exploits other nations. These perennial idols prohibit multiculturalism through myths of manifest destiny and social Darwinism. Their entrance into religion is indicative of commandeering the voice of religion for the state's propaganda. Religious practice in this condition prohibits prophetic denunciation. It is limited to individuals or small communities of faith.

*Idolatry is the entrance of self-induced death into the public sphere. It is when the church supports the state without critique or morals.*

The alternative practices of a Christian community need to reflect values that replace the intrusion of the external forces of the powers. It is not my goal to identify ethical values.[2] Ethical values are important and not to be neglected, but in the process of emphasizing ethical values Christian response has been merely reactive to the culture rather than intentionally subversive and wise. In the community where I lived prior to moving to the Philippines, ethical values focused on broad, theologically based pedagogue rather than divisive issues. This does not exclude conversation about those issues. However, when culturally divisive issues are approached, critical thought is used to help all concerned enter into a learning process rather than immediate dogmatism.

---

1. These perennial idols are displayed in numerous passages throughout the OT prophets. The principal exposure of these idols is in Deuteronomy's commentary in chapters 6–11 on the Decalogue; 7:17 (militarism); 8:17 (materialism); and 9:4 (nationalism).

2. Christian values reflect the teachings of Jesus. It is my position that providing an education to all persons within a given church community is a priority value. God does not leave his children foolish; God is a teacher of goodness.

## PERENNIAL IDOLS

Although I long for the establishment of alternative practices, practices that can subvert the popular culture, I fear it is too little, too late. The church in America has failed to resist the culture through communal ecclesia. The mass appeal of electronic mediums for storytelling has replaced the smaller venue of cultural storytelling belonging to the family and to the fellowship of the Christian community. Storytelling within a family and communal group contributes to identity formation in children and in the incorporation of persons joining the group or ecclesia.

*I am fond of saying, "Storytellers rule the world."*

This natural aspect of culture must be recovered and at this point should be viewed as a resistant effort, resistant to a dominating technology that has invaded our humanity with its permeating intrusion into our cultural ethos and identity formation. The alternative cultural practice of communal storytelling forms a healthy cultural ethos and identity because it is a truly social activity. Likewise the alternative community's educational paradigm should resist the culture. The institutional church has failed to value an education that assists in the development of Christlike persons; it has been replaced with institutionalized systems that make *good citizens* instead of wise believers.

At Global Outreach Developments International, my son Gregg has written numerous one-acts, plays, and a musical as part of an alternative response to the media dominance that feeds us stories embedded in the erring sociopolitical fabric of our society. Throughout the years I have made storytelling a part of my classroom practice. We also intentionally share stories during holiday dinners, even requiring my grandchildren to participate. The G. O. D. regional development teams gather to share stories often.

The implosion of American culture is evident in the growing dissatisfaction of the populace expressed in the national politic. At the core is a dispute over values of moral, ethical, and ideological claims for governing humanity. Historically, this state of affairs is indicative of either a collapse, followed by a restructuring that will render US influence in the world less powerful, or the powers use propaganda, subvert democratic values, and resort to force. This use of force is to continue the distracting power of an unending conflict that will require the United States to go to war. Any protracted war policy with global impact will eventually bring about a full-blown effort to defeat the enemy; this is the nature of response for an empire.

War is most likely because the industrial military complex allows the billionaire class to continue their accumulation of wealth. Profiting from war is both a moral and legal issue; more importantly it is a theological issue. As a moral issue, profiteering from war is *blood money*; it is wealth achieved without any redeeming value. It is offensive to the senses that a person or company should profit from the blood of the sons and daughters of a people. The failure of the church to address such a systemic evil through preaching and protest is indicative of her failure.

*The theological position of Christian faith is that profiteering from war is immoral and must be regulated with written laws that completely prohibit any aspect of military effort from being profitable for any individual, corporation, or state.*

War is a business. Profiting from war demonstrates that it is a business. It militarizes culture and leads to corruption in economic affairs both at home and in relation to other nation-states. This is so because war demands energy, fear, and challenge in order to require that some lose their lives, and so the sacredness of life is lost to the call of war. Law is built upon the value of human life. War resists law. For this reason, law to prevent the descent into war must govern all that relates to the practice of war.

War includes a restriction on democratic values, or uses ideologies of nationalism and the power of propaganda to acquire *manufactured consent* from the populace. War is the business of the powerful; it should be resisted both culturally and legally.

As a theologian, I understand that war is a disturbing reality that God tolerates because God cannot stop us from warring unless God uses force. God desires to teach, to redeem, for us to be reconciled with our Creator. I also understand from the perspective of anthropological theology that Scripture reveals humanity to be self-destructive and subject to moments of madness that erupt in war, war that kills indiscriminately and acts with unrestrained force to establish one sociocultural group as supreme.

It is my sense of reality that our involvement in protracted wars will erupt in a more violent, maddening use of military force. As an empire with the most powerful military force the world has ever seen, the temptation for abuse in order to provide profit for a few is already rampant across the earth.

As police forces are faced with military-type attacks of terror, they require military equipment and training. The end of a militarized state is the use of its forces against its own citizens. The idol of militarism strikes deep into the fabric of all of life. The recruitment of children into the US culture of war begins with absurd tactics like the USMC's practice of sponsoring a "devil pups" camp. The US military's access to public high schools through ROTC programs and other recruitment activity is an intolerable stain on the morality of American culture in relation to minor children. If not halted, cultural militarization can so infest the social fabric that the government itself no longer functions except through the actions of the military.

It is my prayer that collapse and restructuring in the US will occur rather than war. It is my hope that somehow the power of Christian faith will turn the culture of America from its loss of moral values, from its manufactured media culture, from war to peace.

*The unending consumption of the earth's resources by the tower-building capitalists of the world cannot endure with the realities that make for peace.*

On the US political front, the GOP is a threat to all peoples everywhere and to the US citizenry. The progressives are closer to reflecting Christian values through seeking a less-militarized nation, a focus on preserving the environment, and ensuring social responsibility for the oppressed and society's weakest members.

Those of us who know Christ and seek to continue the call of Jesus to establish the reign of God in humanity must not become hopeless or lose ourselves in a debilitating fear. Rather, we must accept that the world is not going to continue on as it is. It is our voices that must wrestle with the culture and stand for truth. We have today, and today we can speak for God through works of love. We can be agents of peace and work with fervor for a resurgence of Christian faith that is free from the trappings of a failed culture or from the trappings of hope in a political solution.

*The immediate moment calls for prophetic denunciation, for resistance to evil when evil is most imminently present.*

It is unwise for the people of God to ignore the immoral weaponry built up in our national stockpiles. If the *dogs of war* are released, it is imperative that all who hold faith in Jesus speak boldly against the use of nuclear weapons. A generation goes and a generation comes, but humanity remains the same. There is no natural evolving of the human species into better persons. The only source for real change in humanity is the people of God, the faithful who live as aliens and strangers in a world where wheat and tare, good and evil, exist side by side (Matt 13:24–42).

I cannot accept that the sign acts of the Berrigan brothers were in vain.[3] Their voice still resonates across the generations to touch us in the present. We have become lethargic in relation to the existence of these weapons. We suppose their use will never occur, that our leaders would not utilize these weapons of mass destruction. We are mistaken.

The US has produced an empire through cultural colonization via a network of nearly 800 military bases in over seventy nations.[4] US military bases reflect the capitalist materialism of life in America through modern housing facilities for its personnel. The housing alone is impressive, but the bases include the construction of world-class malls, golf courses and other recreational facilities. All this voices the power and proposes the superiority of the American way of life. It is an overwhelming display of power capped off with military weaponry unlike the world has ever seen. The military bases with naval ports also boast the intimidating size of modern aircraft carriers and the unknown whereabouts of US nuclear submarines.

The imposing power of the US military supports the invested interests of US corporations in other nations to ensure that the flow of goods to maintain the American way of life is not disrupted. This activity goes on without concern for the welfare of the citizens in these nations.

The US military, supported via the US government, trains Latin American military personnel and trained the President of The Gambia. This activity is infamously known to produce the war criminals and dictators we all abhor. WHINSEC, or the School of the Americas, is located at Ft. Benning, Georgia.[5] That the American news media has ignored this activity is indicative of the interests of their owners; the rich stick together.

The denunciation of war as inconsistent with Christian faith is an act of resistance. Ignoring the suspension of life's sacredness is the guiding immorality of war. It is not wise to ignore humanity's propensity for war. War interrupts life, interrupts all our plans.

---

3. See Berrigan, *To Dwell in Peace*, 290.
4. See Vine, *Base Nation*, 6–7.
5. See Gill, *School of the Americas*.

*War is an eruption of madness, it is self-destruction, it is indicative of a lack of intelligence.*

War is an act against God because it licenses the wholesale killing of human beings who bear the image of God. Christian faith must never close its eyes to the ever-threatening propensity of the powers to fall prey to their own institutional machinations and spiral into the madness of war.

*We ignore war at our own peril.*

The guiding ethic of Scripture, through the most complex situations of life in God's creation, is the preservation of life. As salt, our preserving acts of establishing cultural practices that contend with accepted norms is essential for change. For the practitioners of Christianity these are internal acts, like communal storytelling and an alternative education that is free of indoctrination or programmatic weakness.

The external act of denunciation, of exposing the flawed thinking that leads to militarization and war, is a matter of love that cannot be silenced. It is the cry of God to an erring humanity; it is the cry of God embodied in God's children.

## CHERUBS AND A FLAMING SWORD AT EDEN'S ENTRANCE

The winged cherubim of scriptural imagery, positioned over the mercy seat of the ark, indicate the presence of Yahweh as a listening respondent to the intercession of Moses. In concert with the flaming sword, the imagery of the cherubim suggests God is listening for the absence of the cries for war, listening for the absence of the noise of war in the world of men. I will explain.

I have often wondered over the use of a sword to guard the return into the garden of God. Of course the sword as imagery takes on the power of speech in the New Testament. Yet, the sword is a human invention used for killing others, and during the writing of the Bible was every soldier's weapon. The imagery of the flaming sword at the garden recognizes the two most potent weapons of war, fire and the blade. These components of war prohibit our entrance into the garden. The flourishing garden where the voice of God walks with humanity is unattainable as long as humanity practices war.

# The Consuming Idol of Militarism

*Humanity's violence against one another is indicative of our war with God.*

It is the speech of denunciation belonging to God's children that exposes the madness of warring. We replace the sword of war, of death, with the speech of peace, of life. Our words must cut sharply into the ideologies of normalcy and inevitability on which war is justified, and burn away, via the truth, the powers that consume us through militarism.

# Economics in Theological Thought

Money: Man's Invention

*Theology—economy*
*Endless accumulation*
*Appropriation without morals*
*Making legal—systemic suffering of the poor*
*Self-destructive abuse devouring humanity*
*Where is God?*

## INTRODUCTION

I WILL APPROACH THIS subject from the recognition that the study of economic systems requires the thought of theology, the demands of justice, the critique of philosophy, and the regulation of law, so that a well-informed person can speak about economics in a way that is healing to the people of the world. The globalization of economics has heightened the impact of our monetized world by distributing power to persons that govern the earth's resources and yet are not elected officials. Elected officials are to be held accountable to the people and the law, but in the case of billionaires, their power is not drawn from the state and the law is on their side rather than the demands of justice.

Billionaires and corporate executives have become the gods of the earth with personal wealth, power, and influence that disallow the workings of democracy. The economic holdings of these persons are transnational and rule over the land and the labor of humanity at large. The endless appropriation of wealth present in our economic systems is inconsistent with Scripture and indicative of an evil that produces more pain and suffering in the world than war.

## A SUMMARY ON SCRIPTURAL TEACHING FOR JUST ECONOMICS

### Foundational Teachings from the Mythopoeic Stories of Genesis

The story of Cain, who commits the first murder and the first act of fratricide, is Scripture's first critique on economic development, development that is dependent upon the building of the first city. A theology of the city begins with this ideology: cities are built on murder. Cities require economic exchange so that tax can be accumulated even on perishable items or temporary services such as labor. The city must be built, must be maintained, and as an ideology it supports a broken ethic that presents the survival of the city as more important than its citizens. On the other hand cities give birth to hospitals and universities and a home for the arts, a place for painters and thespians, for intellectuals, poets, and philosophers, for inventors and scientists. Yet at the heart of the city lies the driving power of its growth, which is the abstract value placed on human production and participation in society. The lack of communal ethics and the anonymity of the city aids the social stratification that opposes the egalitarian claims of the preceding creation narratives where every person bears the image of God and every human life is sacred (even Cain's).

The story of the "sons of god" and the "fallen ones" of Genesis 6 is about the end of social stratification, meaning social stratification is a self-destructive practice. The billionaire class (of Genesis 6) take women for purposes of multiplying their seed. This is their attempt at eternal life, to be remembered as fathering superior human beings. Women are merely for breeding and selected based upon their beauty, though it is feasible to also include height and intelligence. The "sons of god," or "fallen ones," through longevity have acquired wealth and power. They are the beneficiaries of the cities and follow the way of Cain. The violence of social stratification, of powerful men abusing women, of taking many women in order to ensure the earth is filled with their seed, is a form of eugenics (breeding) and it all results in the earth's rejection of humanity's violence—the flood.[1]

1. *Mabbul* is the Hebrew word for the flood and is applied to the eruption of chaotic

The final story in the collection of Genesis 1–11 is the tower-building enterprise of humanity to unite collectively and withstand the hostility of the world. Eve reached for the fruit and defied the structures of reality; humanity reaches for the stars in an effort to escape their groundedness rather than receive life as a gift from God. The first couple's misplaced effort to achieve godlikeness, to be qualified as spirit, was halted by God (the entrance of death).

God's design for humanity is in our diversity. Diversity is maintained through the limits of life that produce language. Language is culturally influenced; language and culture are complicated and resist the empire-building plans of humanity so the place is called Babel (Babylon). Theologically the story asserts that all empires fail. Humanity cannot be united as one, and all attempts to make this so will collapse economically or through warring or both. Failure to respect God's diversity in humanity is anti-Christ. Crossing borders is to be an act of peace, not power.[2]

## THE ECONOMICS OF MOSES

It is apparent in Deuteronomy 15 that Moses recognized the endless appropriation of wealth to be as problematic and unhealthy for a people as unending debt. Wealth divides human beings and families, and divides toward destruction; forgiveness unites human beings and families, and it heals. Of course indebtedness and poverty are the result of numerous causes. So Moses follows up his thought in the first three verses of Deuteronomy 15 with a command that the constant effort to abolish poverty is to work toward *no poor among you* (Deut. 15:4), meaning a just society is to provide more than a safety net; they are responsible to share the wealth of

---

waters. The mythopoeic stories of Genesis culminate in the rejection of humanity's path for living. God, in the stories, is the creator who structured reality in a way that rejects the way of humanity. So, God is the originator of the *mabbul*. However, the theological message that links to redemption is that God saves humanity in spite of their violence and in spite of their self-destructive ways lets them live. It is the redemptive work of God that follows. It is the story of God entering history through Abraham and his descendants to reveal God's desire for humanity and show us the way.

2. Crossing borders without intent to harm is taught in the story of Jacob and his father-in-law, Laban. A pile of rocks represents a promise that, although separated, they will not cross to one another's location to cause harm. This is one of the major lessons in the Jacob narratives.

the land with all members so that the economic system can be set aside and resources provided for people regardless of ability to pay.

As Deuteronomy 15 unfolds further, Moses portrays an economic policy where lending to people who are not members of Israel is permitted. However, they are not to indebt themselves as an economic power to other nation-states. The ability to accomplish this feat is dependent upon Israel's obedience to abolish poverty through social structures of debt forgiveness and sharing the resources of the land. Land is God's gift and humanity's inheritance, and there is enough for everyone. Sharing is an ethic for living that brings God's blessing. Within the heart of this passage is the inclusion of others into Israel's economic practices and sharing if those persons recognize Israel's God. It is also within the heart of the passage to claim that the endless indebting of other peoples is inconsistent with Israel's God. Scripture always leaves room for human beings to work out their decision-making processes free from the exercise of legal dialectics. The chapter continues to encourage with warning and blessing.

*It is theologically correct to say that every economic decision is an ethical decision to be made in relation to others.*

Moses declares that God is watching each person's heart concerning his or her use of money. He warns them not to hold back lending because the appointed time for debt forgiveness of every seven years is near. The fight against poverty in Deuteronomy is perennial. This suggests that the law is insufficient because it allows for indebtedness to last up to seven years when God would prefer that we learned to live without indebting one another.

Employees were to be treated with dignity and contracted labor (slave or servant) must come to an end. In only seven years, a person, if they so chose, was to be blessed enough as to be able to go out and start their own self-sustaining living. The boss or employer was to treat his/her contract servants so well that they would voluntarily choose to stay and serve their entire lives. The seven years was to serve and choose to either be an apprenticeship blessed with the ability to live apart from their employer, or a permanent opportunity to work for a human being of kindness and exceptional managerial skills.

PERENNIAL IDOLS

## THE PROPHETS AND GOD'S VIEW ON EXCESS

The prophets demand justice and they do not explain how to implement it. They speak from the vantage point of God. Poverty is oppression and regardless of how one becomes poor, the wealthy are held accountable for the state of the poor. The prophets suffer from the call to speak when darkness is all around and before judgment arrives. They are salt and light, vestiges of hope and purveyors of doom. The pathos of God overcomes them and their speech is electric, radical, immediate, and without diplomacy or respect to the powerful. I will offer a few examples:

Amos rebukes the excessive living of Israel:

> *Thus says the LORD:*
> *For three transgressions of Israel,*
> *and for four, I will not revoke the punishment;*
> *because they sell the righteous for silver,*
> *and the needy for a pair of sandals—*
> *they who trample the head of the poor into the dust of the earth,*
> *and push the afflicted out of the way.*
> *(Amos 2:6–7b)*

Amos rebukes excessive living:

> *Alas for those who lie on beds of ivory,*
> *and lounge on their couches,*
> *and eat lambs from the flock,*
> *and calves from the stall;*
> *who sing idle songs to the sound of the harp,*
> *and like David improvise on instruments of music;*
> *who drink wine from bowls,*
> *and anoint themselves with the finest oils.*
> *(Amos 6:4–6)*

Jeremiah warns of the economic entrapment of the innocent:

> *For scoundrels are found among my people;*
> *they take over the goods of others.*
> *Like fowlers they set a trap;*
> *they catch human beings.*
> *Like a cage full of birds,*
> *their houses are full of treachery;*
> *therefore they have become great and rich,*
> *they have grown fat and sleek.*
> *They know no limits in deeds of wickedness;*

> *they do not judge with justice*
> *the cause of the orphan, to make it prosper,*
> *and they do not defend the rights of the needy.*
> *(Jer 5:26–28)*

## JESUS' PHILOSOPHICAL THEOLOGY ON MONEY

Jesus' vision of God, his grasp of the reign of God, of the existential facets of eternal life, of God's rest, and of the way of God for humanity, all culminate in Paul's understanding of being *in Christ*. It is from this reality that Jesus speaks the following words on money:

> *No man can serve two masters:*
> *for either he will hate the one, and love the other;*
> *or else he will hold to the one, and despise the other.*
> *Ye cannot serve God and mammon.*
> *(Matt 6:24)*

Jesus offers an aphorism that reflects the consummation of a theological statement on economics as money. Jesus presents the power of money as an invading reality on human beings, invading because money competes with God as a voice that claims it is essential for life, even for love. Jesus' portrayal of God and mammon as masters requires the servant to be obedient; we learn the identity of the two masters in the last line. Love is the appropriate way to relate to God, therefore, since mammon competes as a master, then hate is the appropriate way to relate to money. In parallel lines, Jesus drives his point with synonymous emotions of love and (hold to) devotion or hate and despise. In the final line, Jesus personifies money as mammon and places God alongside mammon.

Money is a human invention, an abstract reality that equates the value of a human being's life with metal (and paper, even digits in a computer). The person that loves God must learn to hate the power of money that rules over humanity. Jesus mocked money by paying taxes out of a fish's mouth. God created the fish, which brings life and nourishment, but a coin is an image bearing power in conflict with the Decalogue. Jesus exposed the Pharisees who loved the image-bearing coin of Caesar and quickly displayed their coin when seeking to indict Jesus for a crime against the empire.

*How to hate money* is a legitimate Christian concern. Teaching people to hate money in a way that produces life in spite of the presence and imposed need for money is a Christian activity.

John the Revelator presents money as a consuming power ready to imprison the entire world in its grip, a power that halts bartering, stops sharing, demands payment, and requires life for failing to possess its power.

## A MONETIZED WORLD

## Special Economic Zones and Exploited Labor

SEZs, or special economic zones, are areas within both developing (poorer) nations and developed nations, where foreign investors are enticed with special regulations that are different from the rest of the host nation. These special regulations include tax incentives and lower tariffs. In these zones corporations avoid direct accountability for labor law violations through the use of subcontractors and employee labor contracts. Economic zone businesses seek to establish an environment free from labor law implementation.

Economic zone terminology identifies EPZs (export processing zones) as regimes. This authoritarian term is also applied to the governance of employees. These types of free-trade zones (FTZs) all offer business incentives to foreign corporations. FTZs offer the suspension of a nation's laws for the courting of international commerce and creates areas where the presence of global capitalism functions under regulations that can be negotiated and benefit the corporation without concern for the welfare of the host nation's people. SEZs are known to be labor-intensive areas of production.

In nations like the Philippines and Panama, former US military bases possess the natural isolation and infrastructure that is particularly inviting to foreign investors. China's use of economic zones includes ports, cities, and an entire province. There are over 4,300 economic zones in the world; this number represents the attempt of developing nations to attract global capital and business. Not all zones are successful and SEZ failure results in closure. The success of SEZs in China has come at the expense of exploited labor. This was also so for the temporary success of the Hanjin corporation in Subic Bay, Philippines.

Hanjin's shipbuilding operation in Subic was owned by the South Korean conglomerate HHIC (Hanjin Heavy Industries Corporation) and includes Korean Air. In February 2006, the Hanjin Corporation began their shipbuilding business in the Philippines. The shipbuilding enterprise employed over 26,000 persons and was adding employees in the thousands. It was the fourth-largest shipbuilding business in the world.

The economic zone in Subic was managed by the SBMA (Subic Bay Metropolitan Authority). The former US military base is a sprawling 262 square miles of prime land surrounding the deep-water port. The two major former US bases of Clark and Subic are both designated economic zones and are connected by a Japanese-built expressway that allows ease of travel whether driving from Manila or from one zone to the other. Public transportation (buses and jeepnees) and those unable to pay the expressway fee must use the winding roads that pass through the many towns lining the countryside.

The neighboring city of Olongapo lacks any developmental evidence of benefit from the wealth held in the economic zone or from the prosperity of the Hanjin shipyard. The economic zone serves as a getaway for the wealthy. The SBMA hosts two zoos, zip-line rides, a Sea World-like park, a world-class mall, and multiple warehouse-type shopping centers with food that most Filipino people cannot afford. Former military officer housing is leased and rented by the SBMA and sublet by leases. On the SBMA are first-class restaurants and a marina for yachts. The majority of the 222,000 people of Olongapo cannot afford to eat on the economic zone.

Prostitution in the area was first established to service the troops of the US military. The new visiting forces agreement is sure to increase the sale of women that takes place on both sides of the river that separates the economic zone from Olongapo and Subic Zambales. The economy of the area has not changed enough to rid the area of the blight of prostitution brought on by poverty and maintained by the excess wealth of a few and in particular promulgated by retired US servicemen.

The HHIC (Hanjin) shipyard in Subic achieved 5 billion dollars in sales in five years. The shipyard sits on a 200-hectare area and its estimated value is 1.7 billion dollars. Yet the wage (2015) of a Filipino shipbuilder (welder) was only ninety-four cents per hour. It is difficult to nail down the net income of the HHIC shipyard, as information concerning their use of subcontractors and statements of income is not readily available. However, Hanjin flourished for a while, and it is certain that lots of money was made. The investment of Hanjin was recovered in four years; at this rate a minimum estimated net profit would be around $300 million per year.

Unfortunately, the cost in human suffering for the success of Hanjin's shipyard was borne by Filipino workers who were not paid a living wage.

Hanjin's shipyard had difficulty keeping their shipbuilding employees. During my times working in the Subic Zambales area, I noted that I continually met local men who had been schooled as welders, but left Hanjin. Their complaints included unsafe working conditions, failure to receive a copy of the employee contract they were required to sign, and being coerced into working double 10-hour shifts. All of these men expressed that the attitude of the Koreans toward Filipinos was one of superiority.

There are nineteen subcontractors that manage the workers. These employee management firms serve as a buffer for any liability by Hanjin. Technically the employees work for the management firms. After completing their training, the workers' pay is attached with a 3 percent deduction to cover their training expenses. One-fourth of their pay is spent on bus fees or other forms of transportation to get to and from the shipyard. At ninety-four cents per hour, it is apparent that providing a living wage was not the goal of Hanjin.

The employee management companies imported young men from across the archipelago to work at Hanjin. These young men could not speak the local dialect, were separated from their families, and often did not even know how to operate an ATM (their paychecks came in the form of electronic deposits). When arriving, they were placed in the former Quonset hut housing used by US Marines. Ultimately the employees paid for their training and housing and were subject to signing a five-year contract without knowing the challenges and conditions they would work under. They were also required to sign a document stating they were responsible for their own safety.

In my exposure to the Korean community it was apparent they viewed the Filipino populace as people unequal to Koreans. The evangelical Korean church did not see the Filipino populace as persons to be served with the benefits of education. Korean cultural ideology of superiority over Filipinos is present in the complaints of Hanjin's Filipino employees. Since its inception, the shipyard's Filipino employees complained of mistreatment, with charges including being hit in the head with a Maglite, as well as being kicked and punched by Korean bosses. Koreans have also entered the sex industry in the Philippines and Korean-owned bars for Korean sex tourists are common in Angeles City and other areas of concentrated sex tourism.[3]

---

3. My personal knowledge of the sex industry in Zambales and Angeles city is from

As of September 2014, thirty-eight Filipino workers have died in accidents at the Hanjin facility. Their families receive a payment of 85,000 pesos (around $2,000). The money is released after family members sign documents releasing Hanjin from all responsibility. The number of men injured passed 5,000 in 2009. Still the Filipino workers do not have government representation for workers' rights. Filipino workers attempted to unionize with their organization Samahan, but were refused registration with DOLE (Department of Labor Employment).

## BORN IN DEBT

*Across the earth, millions are born debtors, their lives set on a course of suffering, their nation is a debtor nation and their lives, their land, their economy is determined by a monetized world and a few nations who hold them hostage.*

Not all debtor nations are poor. However, poor nations are held in unrelenting debt through programs that inhibit economic growth and cause abject poverty. These programs are the efforts of the IMF and the World Bank to bind a debtor nation to economic policies that allow international corporations access to the nation's resources, including both land and people. The programs were initially referenced as structural adjustment programs (SAP) and later named poverty reduction strategy papers (PRSP). These programs are forced upon a debtor nation through more loans that are provided if the nation adheres to the economic strategy of the PRSP.

International banking systems of the IMF and World Bank serve the political power of economic colonizing by eight nations: France, Germany, Italy, the United kingdom, Japan, the United States, Canada, and Russia, all of who collectively decide the poverty reduction strategies.

The PRSP is a legal device to require that a nation allow more imports, export more of its resources, liberalize its markets for foreign investors, and cut back on social services, including health and education, in order to make payments. The PRSP agreements include requiring the debtor nation to offer public-owned enterprises for sale to international corporations.

---

efforts to help trafficked women escape. On a more positive note, Korean families vacation in Mactan Island (where I live) and Bohol, where they participate in the local economy. Yet, the majority of the Philippine employees in these many resorts remain underpaid. A college graduate working forty-plus hours a week generally receives around $320 per month.

Often G8 nations have withheld aid during times of great need until a debtor nation agreed to the terms of an SAP or the later PRSP.

## In Effect, a Bank Runs the Whole World

Debtor nations held in the bondage of debt are unable to produce or use the technology to compete with developing nations. For example, a debtor nation is required to ship its unprocessed lumber, and along the way the lumber must be processed in a developed nation and the processing adds more to the cost of the lumber than the initial purchase from the developing nations. This kind of activity keeps the wealthy nation rich and powerful and the debtor nation subject to exploitation and instability. The instability is not limited to economics, but is felt inwardly as well because the people suffer and seek change in their government.

The poverty so easily viewed across Africa, Central and South America, and parts of Asia, all from the window of a jetliner, is indicative of a world of injustice. The god named mammon rules the world from ivory towers. The alleged complexity of the global economic system is all a façade to allow academics to write lengthy studies on how to end poverty through a failed system of indebtedness. The world has become a macrocosm reflective of Egypt, and Goshen is the home of God's people.

Moses understood a long time ago that a people living in a monetized world must learn to forgive debt—in particular the debt of the poor. Moses understood that a people seeking to be a model for others would flourish through the practice of debt forgiveness within their own borders and be able to loan to other nations. I think Moses knew that such a nation would be able to forgive debt to another nation that learned to live justly and instituted the Torah legislation of debt forgiveness for their people.

Excessive living is the practice of a person who is disconnected from reality. It is the practice of the rich man who ignored Lazarus and woke up in his tormented state of separation from the father of Israel. Excessive living is unspiritual; it is the enemy of the poor. Always be kind to the poor, to those who work without adequate wages. Leave generous tips, smile, and treat them with dignity and graciousness. God will be blessed.

# The Banality of Evil and the End of a Nation

### The Demonic

*The demonic is without a conscience*
*Fearing the good—bound by absurdity*
*Appears suddenly like a disruptive illness*
*Breeding hate—its object is always humanity*
*Promising to repair the world—but only for the ruthless elite*
*Nationalism its lover—murder its sensuous offspring*

THE BANALITY OF EVIL is a phrase used by Hannah Arendt. It is the subtitle for one of her books, *Eichmann in Jerusalem: A Report on the Banality of Evil*. She uses the life of Eichmann and his trial to display the banality of evil in an indifferent and unprincipled man. The inept, thoughtless Eichmann exemplified the power of systemic structures of evil that normalize intolerable genocidal murder without resistance from the concept of good people. We like to think that good people are numerous in every society and will resist intolerable evil, but we have learned through the holocaust that this is not so.

We cannot depend upon this concept of good people to halt the runaway powers of systemic evil in society, evil rooted deeply in history, funneling up through culture like a volcanic eruption that leaves the ashes of human beings spread across the earth. Our ancient ancestors mythologized this reality as gods and demons. They made peace with the reality of evil by deifying the state apparatus. We still do the same.

In the gospels the defeat of these powers took place through the overcoming life of Jesus, whose resurrection affirmed all of his teaching. It is apparent we have not learned the lessons of the gospel. Paul the apostle was less prone to using the mythological view for his instruction on reality than Jesus did in the Gospels. Paul identifies the principalities and powers of the air as systemic injustice, as evil in both the political sphere and the religious. The participating powers in the death of Jesus include empire, the military, the state, the crowd, the political, the religious, and the betrayal of friends who fled in fear when these powers acted against Jesus. In my thought, the betrayal of Jesus' disciples was participatory because they did not resist. When we are confronted with evil, resistance is not an option, but a moral imperative:

> *He disarmed the rulers and authorities and made a public example*
> *of them, triumphing over them in it.*
> *(Col 2:15)*

Briefly, Jesus disarmed the systemic structures of evil through his teaching, innocence, resurrection, nonviolent resistance, and the Spirit. In the crucifixion of Jesus, all forms of human governance are exposed as lacking the awareness and power to resist evil, unless they grasp the message of the cross. In the present age, large cultural enclaves of Christianity and the Christian message have been swallowed up in clerical religion and lost to the idols of the state: militarism, materialism, and nationalism. The lack of resistance is indicative of a failure to grasp the meaning, the message of the cross.

This being said, it is my purpose in this piece to expose the underlying structures of evil in both soul and society. Evil creeps into the soul through social structures that bring order into a hostile world where both nature and humanity pose threats to humanity. Yet humanity's efforts to bring order fail, and the grandest enterprise for governing or producing ethical human beings who resist evil continually fails and evil erupts on multiple fronts like Leviathan from the sea to permeate reality with corruption.

Belief in the personification of evil as a living entity negates human responsibility to resist, to choose; it only serves ignorance and exonerates humanity's culpability for the reality of evil. Lest some think that we have progressed, I will state clearly: progressive human development is a myth that ignores the permeating presence of systemic and institutional evil that continues to bind us like a chained demoniac.

# The Banality of Evil and the End of a Nation

*And we know that we are of God, and the whole world lies in wickedness.*
*(1 John 5:19)*

A discerning, intelligent sensitivity to evil resonated in the prophets. The insensitivity to evil that is resident in American society is at the root of the eruptions of evil present in the US and across the globe. I will be more precise and dig deeper into the seething monster that lives beneath the surface of our niceties. First, I will address the concept of sacrifice as applied to those who lose their lives to the machinations of war.

I will begin with the erring, populous Christian view of sacrifice (PSA Theory) that has missed the irrational display of love and its startling exposure of human evil revealed in the death of Jesus. God joined humanity (*kenosis*) and met our need for God to speak to us as one of us, met our need for God to respect our struggles for existence, and loved us to death. Jesus died because humanity murdered God. We silence God's voice every day and refuse to give ourselves to the kind of love displayed in God on a cross.

The sacrifice of human life is murder. In order to displace vengeance from an object, namely *a person,* Levitical religion used animals, an act that challenged the constant refrain of Israel's death penalty.[1] The view of Jesus' death as a religious sacrifice ends the sacrificing of animals because it exposes the failings of religious sacrifice; they are unable to change the practitioner. Because Jesus' death is followed by his resurrection, followed by the giving of God's Spirit, humanity can be set on a course free from the temporary release of evil's machinations that religious sacrifice temporarily appeased. Sin is never personal; it is always relational:

> *...but visiting the iniquity of the parents*
> *upon the children...*
> *(Exod 34:7d)*

*Sin is never merely an individual matter; it is always relational, with repercussions that reach into the generations.*
*The celebration of sin produces the unrecognized power that reduces evil to banality.*

---

1. Vengeance belongs to God and God is not vengeful. Sin is repercussive. Sin's effects and the effects of the perennial idols of humanity are often perceived as God being vengeful. PSA theory is built upon the ideology of vengeance and not God's mercy or life-giving justice.

# PERENNIAL IDOLS

The individualizing of sin, the individualizing of salvation, without recognition of their role in all of humanity is an intolerable reduction of theological truth. It is a subtle evil that has affected the success of the gospel to produce a people with a Spirit-inspired understanding of and sensitivity to evil.

The grand evils that go unrecognized or unacknowledged are humanity's war against the voice of God in creation, the moral conscience, the message of the cross, and the Spirit of God, the Spirit who calls all of us to a banquet of life. This war is played out on the field of human history where endless displays of self-destruction become normalized activities accomplished blasphemously in the name of God. When we are at war with our brother (Abel) we are at war with God. When we do not understand that God is not at war with us but lay his multicolored bow in the sky exposing its string to the ground, God is saying "I will not allow Leviathan to overcome humanity but let them live in spite of their violence."[2]

In order to stop humanity's collective violence, God would need to kill, to use force to stop us, and yet he refuses. The death of the Egyptian firstborn and the firstborn animals is a controlled, and never to be repeated, lesson of God's power to stop those who would kill the innocent. Yet, the Pharaoh chose to pursue the slaves into the sea and be swallowed up in the waters of Leviathan. The rulers of the world are at war with God; they will not let go of their power to rule over humanity, they prefer the evil machinations of war. War is madness.

Hope is present in the communal ecclesia, the people of God who understand the systemic powers of evil and expose them in their most

---

2. It is important that we do not lose the distinctly communicative symbol of the rainbow to the metaphysical myth of sexuality that claims God created people to be homosexual. Homosexuality is the end of life. The lack of sexual ethics present in the current acceptance of homosexuality is unhealthy. The failure to acknowledge the societal ramifications by normalizing sexuality without ethically identifiable behavior is a path of self-destruction. The rainbow is a symbol of mercy, not accommodation and approval. Yet, we must acknowledge that hatred for gender-confused persons is evil and an intolerable response. Love and empathy are the Christians" first response and present as we wrestle with our brothers and sisters for light, peace, understanding, grace, and ethical sexual behavior.

The perennial idols and their institutional leaders bring more harm to the world than homosexuality. Likewise, sexual abuse, and the sex industry that caters to the imperial armies of the world, is more damaging to humanity than the presence of homosexual persons in a given society. The presence of homosexuality is increased where the sex industry is operating. Sex carries an enormous potential for good; it also possesses enormous potential for harm.

subtle manifestations. The first lie of systemic evil is that war is *inevitable*. Then there is the idea of honorable sacrifice that covers over and distracts from the reason wars are fought: the powerful profit and the populace is deceived, always deceived. The consuming idol of militarism is present in the evil that fills the world with war memorials where the worship of the dead as a sacrifice to the national religion reigns in the place of God.

War memorials always lie (unless they remember the victims). Auschwitz is a fitting memorial for it requires we remember the banality of evil alive in the state apparatus and its servants.

## GOD WANTS A PEOPLE, NOT A NATION-STATE

Personal wealth acquired or kept at the expense of others is evil. The underlying structure of evil present in capitalism is an intolerable compromise of Christian faith. The systemic structures of evil have placed multitudes of Lazarus's children outside the gate of the US economy. Humanity requires social structures free of evil that contribute to the flourishing of life for every person on the entire earth. These structures cannot be a global government; centralizing power is inconsistent with God's multicultural design for human life.[3]

*Love is to remove those structures that birth the need for anyone to sacrifice their life; this is part of the instructive revelation of the cross.*

The failure of any governing entity to educate its citizens in the finer attributes of humanity and enable their citizens to flourish is an evil. The presence of ignorance in any population is the sin of failing structures in the state, in the institutions that deprive some of learning. Education that is geared toward producing good citizens who do not question or challenge the governing powers is not education. Education that leaves young people indebted to the powers of state, banks, and universities is a systemic evil.

Surely hopelessness is the end product of trusting in humanity to cure this illness of sin that permeates our history, our reality, and our lives.

---

3. God's multicultural design for human life resists the establishment of a single language (Gen 10). The nature of linguistic development in the human family avoids totalitarian control over the meaning of language by any single group. The natural boundaries that separate people along with accompanying physical adaptations contribute to separate cultures. A multicultural society would display multiple languages and disallow conformity of dress and personal aesthetics in relation to hairstyles.

Advanced technology and science have not in any way begun to root out the reality of structural evil, they have only hidden it beneath the pale of comfort. Self-destruction defines all our activities. Humanity consumes unrenewable resources from the earth (we sacrifice the earth). Humanity devises weapons that threaten our existence. Hope is found only with the people of God. The need for Christian faith to rise above the impotency exhibited in surrender to the consuming idols of militarism, materialism, and nationalism (ethnocentrism) is urgent.

I care enough about life and the generations to stand and believe that Jesus' faith and teaching can change the world. The loss of Christian faith to perennial idols and the systemic structure of evil in all its banality plagues the present. We are at the precipice of hopelessness like Jeremiah. America's culture is unsustainable. The US as a global power is unsustainable. Institutional Christianity is capsized by idols. We need Christianity.

# The End of Idolatry

## The End of History

*Idolatry ends in madness*
*The spirit of idolatry is human weakness*
*Without God's reign, idols are inevitable*
*Allegiance to rules and ideas*
*Deifying that which is without being*
*Life outside of God is idolatrous*
*God all in all*
*The end of idolatry*

ULTIMATELY ALL IDOLATRY WILL end when God wins. In the meantime there is another end, and it sits in dark contrast to a completed humanity, a humanity embraced into the being of God so that God is all in all. Idolatry is always a failing power ever on a descent into madness. Madness also is the end of idolatry. It erupts in self-destructive powers that kill humanity and poison the ground. Even reason, in all its grandeur and insight, falls prey to idolatry when faith in one God who is love is detracted into any other form of religious thought. Only a monotheism that culminates in the revelation that God is love, that God defines love, and provides the meaning for love, only this kind of monotheism is capable of providing a way of living for humanity that brings peace. A monotheistic religion of love finds God in history and embraces the revelation of God as the abolition, the ultimate end, of idolatry.

Idolatry is the sustained dependence of humanity upon a system or institution that governs through force. The state's claim to sovereignty over human life—the right to kill—is its defining power. The unquestioned right of the state to take life is idolatry and is exhibited in war, in the death penalty, in military conscription, in incarceration, and in laws that do not allow citizens to challenge or critique the state's practice of warring.

The state's development of an economic system that gives rise to a few with power for the endless appropriating of wealth is idolatry. This is so because it creates god-like personas that others admire and seek to emulate as models for what it means to be great. Nation-states naturally develop systems of idolatry, namely pride and sacrifice. Without these they would not be able to maintain the military apparatus.

These idols do not produce, they rob; they do not bring justice, they develop systemic structures of evil and they end in destruction. At the core of idolatry is violence. This is so because violence is self-destructive, it is the absence of God in the world. Idolatry always ends in violence because it is humanity living apart from God, living without faith. Theology understands, and rightly so, that God is multifaceted—God is one, God is a being, God is spirit, God is creator, and so forth. It is also correct to say that God is the spirit who ends violence in the human family.

*The soul that rejects violence receives God into the world.*

The end of idolatry culminates in the end of madness and violence, and idolatry cannot end without being exposed, resisted, and renounced. Yet the very systems that constitute the efforts of humanity to organize life are the idols that end in violence. Until the victory of God is fully arrived, humanity is subject to the need for organized systems that help us live and work together. This is so because human beings are not taught to know the Lord. So, the task is to expose the idolatry and move the organizational effort, or the *ecclesia*, toward the reign of God.

The Scripture teaches that loving God and loving one's neighbor holds the power to bring about the end, or goal, of the Torah. The objects for love are God and human beings. The Hebrews used the word hesed and the Greeks used agape for expressing the love of God. Humanity is the object of God's love. Using the word love for any other purpose outside of loving God and human beings is an unhelpful nuance of the word. The misappropriation of the word "love" is an unfortunate inadequacy in the English language, and in a subtle way is a path to idolatry. *Hesed* and *agape*, in Scripture, provide us with the universal ultimate concerns for every human being and institution: the search for God and care for the life of every human being.

## The End of Idolatry

When institutions of government seek to promote humanitarian responses to the machinations of injustice that produce suffering but do not correct the inherent failures in their systems idolatry is present. The first injustice is the corruption of leaders that takes place when they are unequal servants, that is, their life is more important than those of the populace. This is seen in the accruement of wealth, the concept of greatness, and the building of fortresses for securing their lives against the very violence their actions produce. Christianity is egalitarian and altruistic. Christianity is incompatible with the concepts of self-interest and capitalism.

A leader in pursuit of God, out of love for the outcome when God is found, when God enters the world through acts of love, that leader will not secure his life with wealth attained at the expense of a single human being. This is the Christlike behavior that is to be modeled by every human being and particularly by those who are leaders of faith, of the people of God. We lose our humanity when we exalt any single person or group of human beings as being more valuable than others, or when we devalue the life of another.

*What creates a man like Pharaoh or like any exalted powerful leader?*
*We do.*

To hope in any system to cure humanity's ills is idolatrous. When we all learn how to live, how to love, it will be the end of law. The healing of the world always begins with the single individual who in relationship is never truly an individual. The power of the individual who is connected to history, to others, but bound to love for God, is to heal the world.

The rulers of the world hold power and their position is always fragile. A despot always knows a single voice can be his undoing. For this reason, swift and decisive action is required to silence that one voice. When the voice is one of nonviolence and justice, the machinations of propaganda and concepts of law that resist change are the leader's first line of defense from acting justly. Once or if the leader is allowed by his petty legions of followers to become the law, then simply killing the single voice is accomplished with immediacy and without regard for the thought and feeling of the people.

It is apparent that the greatest enemy in this process of idolatry is the masses of unthinking persons who are taught to love their people above others, and to love their nation, their government, and their leaders.[1] For

---
1. It is idolatrous to love one's nation. To correlate being a good Christian with being

## PERENNIAL IDOLS

this reason, education that develops thinking human beings is the enemy of the state, of all states. In a capitalist-driven democracy, education becomes a banking system of relentless and irrelevant academic exercise. The intellectuals sell out for wealth and power. The goal of education in a declining system is to turn a student into a functioning cog in the public wheel of mass production, not an individual.

Since our individuality is connected to history and family and all that surrounds our life, we need a more nuanced definition or explanation for what constitutes an individual. To support my claims on being an individual, I will use some of the words and thought from Abraham Joshua Heschel, words that he applies to the prophets.[2] An individual holds God and humanity in a single thought at all times. This is a state of being which is accomplished through love for God and humanity. The result is a person who chooses to exemplify the best of all that has formed his or her life, an individual who retains the courage to say *no* to power and not lose their identity to unjust, unethical, or trendy social constructs.

An individual of courage who resists injustice is a spiritually intelligent person. A spiritually intelligent person has learned to depend upon God and to be disappointed by people, while holding onto their own dependency and need for people.

When examining a relationship with another human being or any situation, first identify what you know, then think about all that you do not or cannot know, and then talk with the person, not about them. Listen to them and learn to hear. Try to heal a situation or a person, not pronounce your judgment. Overcome the contentious with wisdom and beware the unjust, they will sacrifice you for their systems and their desires.

An idol is any social or political construct that displaces dependency upon God to a system that justifies social stratification and violence. Social stratification is essential for injustice to be legitimized. The reign of God is an egalitarian power of life-giving Spirit that serves the weak through the strong, and in the process, both are healed.

Idolatry's end is self-destruction because the source of life and goodness has been replaced. As individuals disappear, idolatry abounds and its

---

a good citizen (as in subservient without resisting or questioning) is an error that leads to losing the faith to an idol.

2. A prophet's true greatness is his ability to hold God and man in a single thought. See Heschel, *Prophets*. 25.

power increases until goodness in people is lost to a state of blindness, closing their eyes for the sake of a false peace built on impermanence.

Idolatry's ends are unbridled power, rampant injustice, and the suffering of the poor. Idolatry sacrifices human beings at the altar of Molech, burning children as collateral damage from drone attacks. Idolatry releases the monsters of darkness hidden in systems of law and commemorates the deaths of a people's children to the warring of the state.

# CATEGORY III

# REALITY

# Reality Creation

### The Invitation

*Come create with me*
*Create reality*
*I will watch*
*I will join you*
*Let me help you*
*Life is real*
*Reality is more than you*
*Learn to live, to fail, to die, to rise again*

ALTHOUGH THE APEX OF God's creation is humanity, the creation of reality is a relational process that includes both God and humanity. The creation of reality is seldom considered as something to be in awe of or to be grateful for; it is important to think deeply about reality within the context of possibility and theology.

*Reality is a person's ontological experience of life with other human beings, their perception of God, and the world.*

*Reality is the sphere of both God's presence and absence, of humanity's choices that are either in accord with God or opposed to God's participation in reality.*

*Reality-creation within the limits of existence is always a compromised choice for the powerful.*

Reality is not merely a *result* of God's creative activity; it is a creation of God's. Unlike other aspects of creation, reality remains open to ongoing creative imagination and power. Science and technology utilize creation, whereas individual reality (each person's perceptions and understanding of self) is existential and not essentially subject to the advances of science and technology.

Reality is a realm of possibility. We are made to share with God in the creation of our reality. Reality provides the creature (specifically humanity) an existence that requires they be like God. We are to be like God by participating in the creation of reality through imaginative and faith-filled efforts that demonstrate that the reality of God's reign can be lived and experienced. We are to be like God in love, mercy, and forgiveness or the world will not work, reality will be broken. When we are not like God, reality-creation is marred. Jesus taught that we are to create the reality of the reign of God by doing the works of God.

It is evident in the creation narrative that the image of God is to be lived out within the context of our genders. Image and likeness are not determined by gender but by our common humanity. Further, the failure of a life-honoring relationship between the genders is a marring of the image and likeness:

> *So God created humankind in his image,*
> *in the image of God he created them;*
> *male and female he created them.*
> *(Gen 1:27)*

In the *human condition narrative* (fall narrative), reality as a relational effort accomplished by God and humanity begins with the entrance of sin, sex, and death. Only within the fading memory of childhood can the myth of primal innocence live. Outside the garden, death, with its certainty, wrestles us away from the grandeur of life's gift. However, death insists that life is real, not a dream or a predetermined event, but a choice—because death permeates all of existence and is not just our last breath.

Death is a sobering part of our existence that is in conflict with the godlikeness and image that is given to us beyond the limits of discovery by biological science. Our sense of being is in conflict with death as the final word on life. Human beings cannot accept death as their intended state. We are made to seek God.

> *He has made everything suitable for its time; moreover he has put*
> *a sense of past and future into their minds, yet they cannot find out*
> *what God has done from the beginning to the end.*
> *(Eccl 3:11)*

Death is the absence of God. I think it is for this reason that God is depicted in the story as absent when Eve stands before the tree, and when the violation of the prohibition occurs. The presence of God enters our reality when with faith we bring God into the world by living in an altruistic way.

The inexplicable moment of Jesus' sense of being forsaken while enduring the cross is reflective of God's absence. This is a mystery, for God had become a human being without exception, yet to be human is to die. So, in Christ, God added to God's self the experience of dying.

Spiritual intelligence is to face reality. The failure to face reality and rely upon one's ideological prejudices or instincts, or to simply follow the masses, is a carnal exercise. To face reality as a spiritual person is to accept the relational aspect of humanity with awareness, burden, and culpability. Awareness of history and the present is an educational effort to recognize the personhood of every human being and be concerned about all of humanity. Burden is to feel the weight of empathy in concert with God's love. Culpability is to ask the question: What am I to do? Spiritual intelligence connects the heart with God's will for humanity to live abundantly.

Spirituality is the effort to bring God into the world by aligning one's self with the will of God. The will of God is always conducive to improving and establishing the flourishing of humanity through acts of love. If we form the world in ways which are inconsistent with the goodness of God, then chaos and suffering will follow.

History has no meaning without the presence of suffering and death. Angels have no history, they do not exist; they are but personifications that are used to distance us from being closer to God, or they are momentary *flames of fire—ministering spirits—*that serve to communicate God to us.[1] Occasionally human beings are mistaken for angelic beings.

The suffering we should address in the study of history, for it to be a positive, reality-creating exercise, are stories of goodness lived out in the midst of suffering and death. We must not allow for the stories of martyrs to become historical personages to be adored. We must not allow their lives to become mythical so that their faith and courage are lifted to a place for the dead, rather than a norm for all believers.

Stories or events that explain reality prior to history are myths. Myths are also used to explain our ontological reality. Myths are a form of communication and ideological referencing for understanding reality.

---

1. See Hebrews 2.

# REALITY

History exists as a discipline, or study, in hopes that we might become more than we've been. However history is not always factual when recorded by the powerful. This being said, the powerful create a false narrative that forms reality. So, reality is both created and perceived based upon a person's awareness and education.

The sacralizing of war through remembering the dead as sacrifices for the nation is not history; it is a form of reality-making that perpetuates war. It is a religious exercise that culminates in the worship of the dead. In Christianity, God is the God of the living, not of the dead. Death does not speak the creative word, only God possesses the final word on creation and reality.

Words form reality; they can also form a false reality because people without the knowledge of God are easily swayed toward self-preservation (self-interest). People also fail to understand their role in the creation of reality. We are all responsible for our participation in the creation of reality.

The life of Jesus affirms a difficult fact about reality under God's sun, namely, that the righteous, the innocent, can become victims of humanity's reality that functions in the realm of God's absence. This fact is a part of our reality. Rene Girard touches on this truth in his theory on the scapegoat mechanism.

In our effort to order reality, we miss the anarchic part of reality where God walks on water, hovers over the deep, and allows our faith to be tested. Jacques Ellul explores Christian anarchy well in his writings. Meaning the Christian faith is geared to overcome scapegoating the innocent and to walk into the anarchic without fear. The anarchic is to trust God when the established order is lost to doing what is right. It is to defy the established or deified order of man without yet knowing what God will do. Meaning it is better to do right than to let the scapegoat mechanism bring temporary relief to a broken reality. Scapegoating fails, the need to expel or persecute will resurface and others will be victimized by our unresolved desires.

Human beings suffer at identifying the scapegoat mechanism because it's so universal and culturally engrained. Whenever one individual is identified as the solution for relieving the evasive cause of tension in a group it is certain that the scapegoat mechanism is at play. Of course, this evasive tension can be falsely proclaimed, lacking the perspective of a third disinterested party. It is not the supposed cause of the tension that is the problem, it is the solution to sacrifice a single person through acts of violence that call for exclusion of an innocent person. Innocence is relative in this sense. It is relative to the hidden issues left unresolved by the group. The scapegoat is only a temporary solution to humanity's flaws that exist in any group.

God is a benevolent being of love and violence is not consistent with the reality that God desires humanity to live,in to co-create, to produce—a lived reality accomplished in Christ. At the core of all failed human efforts at forming reality is violence. Christianity is able to develop human beings who mature, choose the risk of suffering and/or death, and are able to give it all rather than succumb to using violence. These are the people who shake existing structures and cause anarchic moments of uncertainty.

Although death devalues life and contributes to humanity's errant reasoning for using violence, Jesus' lived faith demonstrates that we are capable of better, capable through the Spirit of bringing, of manifesting the kingdom of God.

Apocalyptic alarmists have abandoned hope and prefer self-destruction, they choose anarchy not rooted in faith but in demand for God's rescue; I would not be so presumptuous to think that God is incapable of leaving us to destroy ourselves so he can subsequently start over again. Apocalyptic alarmists create a false reality where humanity is incapable of living out the calling of becoming God's children. This is inconsistent with the gospel of good news. It ultimately makes Christianity impotent to change the world. As Christians we have been called to co-create with God the reality of God's reign on earth by being exemplars of Christian faith.

# The Underlying Structures of Reality

The Voice of God

*Are you hiding?*
*But how can you?*
*Are you silent?*
*The echoes of your voice sail the cosmos*
*Enter the heart of humanity*
*And I*
*I search for you to tell me why I am here*
*My heart is unsettled*
*There is more than I see*
*I find you in speech*
*In all you've created*
*I live as though you're watching*
*You're in my every thought*
*I need you O' Lord*

THE UNDERLYING STRUCTURES OF *reality* is a phrase for referencing the relational and physical realities that form and govern our experience of knowing the world as human beings. Some of these structures are cultural while others are universal. We often live aloof from these structures, as though they lack definition or are not easily discernible.

We use words to explain these realities that belong to the human experience. Words evidence our insight into the world and enable us to live beyond instinct. Words are like spirit; they are invisible and have power beyond mere sound. With words we limit and define the world, (our experience of reality). We question and seek answers in our pursuit of understanding how to live. The perennial questions that drive us (Who am I? and Why am I here?) speak to our incompleteness, our need to become.

Our ability to form our own reality with ideological concepts that frame human thought and life continually threatens our need for *shalom*. *Shalom* comes from living in harmony with God and in concert with others.[1] The ability to form our relational reality and challenge the physical limits of reality is both a gift and a curse, or life and death. It is a curse because the relational reality we form with words often lacks the love (justice is governed by love) essential for *shalom*. *Shalom* is blessing (fulfillment) because we can learn to align our creatureliness with the creation and our Godlikeness with Spirit. It is insight working with faith that enables us to overcome instinct and live as both creature and spirit.

The structures of relationally formed reality are a conundrum as stable as God's promises and as fluid as infinite possibility within measurable confines. The physical structures of reality are measurable and calculable, meaning there is differentiation in the creation that forms the natural world, e.g., male and female, animals, sea life, trees, vegetation, ground, earth, the sky, the cosmos.

The Hebrew search for wisdom includes the relational realities constructed in the king's court. This is evident in the book of Proverbs. Proverbs are generally basic pedagogical statements for young people; they are not promises nor are they great insights into reality. For the most part, proverbs are aids for succeeding in a cultural milieu. The basics of the book of Proverbs begin with two simple pieces of instruction; don't be greedy and males must learn to restrain their sexuality. These two acknowledge that the underlying structures of reality are in opposition to greed and unrestrained sexuality. A healthy life for young males requires attentiveness to disciplining these two desires.

To unlock the depth of the compiler or redactor of the book of Proverbs requires a structural reading of the book. Behind apparent cultural misogyny is a message of liberation. For the attentive reader this is explicit in the final chapter where it is a mother who passes on wisdom. The end of a piece of literature is always important and Proverbs' ends with a king taught wisdom by his mother. It includes a theme running throughout Scripture that a woman can raise a good son without the presence of the father.

1. Because God is redemptive, God allows for the disturbance of *shalom*. We too must suffer the disturbance of *shalom* in order to heal the world. The Hebrew phrase *tikkun olam* is an idiom that means "repairing the world." This is our task, our way in which we live and walk, even though we do not see its completion.

# REALITY

*Simplicity is found in a proverb and wisdom is the complexity of pain and experience in the laughter of the one that agrees with the proverb while laughing at its exceptions.*

Creation also takes place within relational reality through words that we speak and use, words that govern over our thoughts and actions (unless we act from instinct or suffer psychosis). We are created in God's image. *God is a relational, redeeming creator who keeps covenant.* These four are indicative of the image of God within human beings. John writes that God is love and this truth is the power behind the four I have listed.[2]

We are co-creators with God or we uncreate God's good world via the *animal* sin. God cannot be redemptive without someone to redeem. Our redemption is a reconciliatory process. We partake in the process of creation and redemption by learning to speak correctly about the world, by speaking correctly to each other, by mixing our speech and actions with grace and mercy amidst a world of chaos where sin has entered many times and its repercussive power lingers like a monster.

We must learn that when we speak with another human being we need to be intentional and compassionate with our words, there is nothing more powerful than words and they should be used for the healing of the broken relational reality we all experience. Perhaps James's admonition on the power of the tongue is primarily written for teachers?

*As we become aware of the structures of reality we should become peacemakers with our words and actions, we should be able to see God in the darkness.*

I think Paul understood this concept when he spoke of the "elemental spirits of the universe," the *stoichea*. I think Martin Luther King Jr. understood this concept when he stated that the moral arc of the universe may swing wide but it swings toward justice. I think the underlying structures of reality reflect the good creation and attest to the marring of the good creation through the impact of sin and death. Death is God's severest judgment; as a structural part of reality it is the most powerful. It speaks the loudest and humanity cannot overcome its power by our own efforts. Yet, death is also a fact of the human condition and not inherited punishment

---

2. The image of God is demonstrated in many ways, including humility. I am not attempting to establish a conclusive or exhaustive list. The list I have compiled is based upon dominant themes found in the OT.

for some primal sin. Ultimately death is the enemy of God because of his love for humanity and the embrace in which he holds us all. In the present, death is an underlying structure of reality and declares that we are not fit to live. Only God's mercy allows us to continue as God seeks to redeem us.

One of the structural elements of the universe that proceeds from God is the biblical theme that our ethical and moral behavior affect the ground from which life proceeds. We take this one for granted, for example, as we pray 2 Chronicles 7:14. This prayer explicitly links moral behavior to the healing of the land. Hosea 4:1–3 teaches that sin dismantles life to the degree that death is not just an end, but also a present power woven into creation. This passage in Hosea also enables us to make the theological statement that our ethical and moral behavior affects the cosmos, the ground, and animal life. This is true in both a physical sense, through ethical use of the earth in relation to humanity, and through a spiritual reality upheld by God.

We are all of the *adamah*, the ground, as was our ancestor, Adam. Our goal is to learn to become life-giving spirits like the *last Adam*, Jesus. I think that as we learn to recognize the underlying structures of reality, we connect with the voice of God that sets the limits and order of existence under the sun. However, God still speaks, particularly to challenge each of us to manifest the spirit of God in the world by being obedient to the revelation of God in Christ. Theology is always ontological because God is a being, is the living God.

*To live in an intelligent relationship with the underlying structures of reality is the dance that moves with the rhythm of life.*

The Hebrew quest for wisdom, for discerning the voice of God through the created order—that is the underlying structural elements of reality—explores the revelation of God in creation and seems to neglect the stories of Israel that contain the revelation of God in Jewish history. Wisdom in the Bible is a form of *natural theology* and avoids the complications of theology drawn from interpreting complex narratives. The pursuit of God through the ideology of monotheism, accompanied by the witness of creation and human experiencem, is a spiritual exercise.

For example, the universal human rejection of death as acceptable, and the desire for life beyond our creaturely limits, testify to the structural reality of how we have been created as human beings. Ecclesiastes 3:11 informs us that God has set in the heart of human beings *ha-olam,* that is, the idea of forever. This single insight is a universal reality experienced by all human beings. It is Hebrew wisdom at work and also is existential reflection. As an underlying structure of humanity's creation, our longing for life without death, our ability to conceive of forever, reflects the reality of a creator, an unseen, self-sustaining God who is without end.

The underlying structure of reality that exists within us as creatures is our relatedness to God through likeness and image; relational, redeeming, creating, and promise-keeping.[3] These structures are guided by the collective reality of the moral conscience, which encompasses each and is to be governed by love. Love is always a gift because it proceeds from God. Yet, like all God's gifts, it can be marred in expression if not governed by moral conscience and insight. In the flux and flow of life it is promise-making and keeping promises that ensure love's faithfulness.

I will offer my own aphorism that is basic pedagogue and identifies underlying structures of reality for all humanity.

*Everyone is afraid and everyone wants to be loved.*

The simplicity of wisdom is reflected in sayings that communicate universal truths about human reality. These sayings are always empowering, instructive, and easy to remember.

## SEXUALITY AND STRUCTURES OF REALITY

The most promising and most harmful aspect of the underlying structures of reality is the role of human sexuality. Sexuality is essential, yet its temporal function grounds each of us in the earth as creatures that are dependent upon an instinctual sexual impulse for our survival. Gender and procreation, male and female, these creaturely structures form the beginnings of the relational reality in which human maturation takes place. Sin, violence, and sexuality are major themes introduced in the creation narratives nearly simultaneously, and enter the world at the same moment. Nakedness and shame both arrive as consequences of violating the initial prohibition to not eat of the tree of the knowledge of good and evil. Although the command to multiply came before this event, any other possibility of imagining sexuality free from the realities of nakedness and shame are removed.

---

3. There are other traits that demonstrate image and likeness. My list is not exhaustive, but is workable. For example, insight over instinct is reflective of likeness and image, as is our discontent with mortality.

# The Underlying Structures of Reality

Shame for sexual misconduct is one of the most damaging realities in life. Shame is an underlying structure of reality.

Sin is always a violation of the underlying structures of reality. Sin is first an existential act of violence against one's self; it is to reach beyond the structures of reality for forbidden fruit in a garden overflowing with the fruit of goodness. Next, sin is an external act that blames the existence of the other because sin is always expressed relationally once existential violence is done to our psyche. Because the initial act of existential violence for violating the structures of reality (reaching beyond for the fruit) and sex (recognition of nakedness) enter the world at the same moment in the Genesis narratives, sex is viewed as incompatible with spirit and a result of our separation from God; yet sex is not sin. Interestingly, the word "sin" is not used in the Genesis narrative until Cain's murder of his brother. However, sex is not spirit and it is the confusion of the two that results in the most heinous religious aberrations. For this reason, sexual restraint is a spiritual discipline and is an underlying structure of reality.

Sexuality, like sin, is related to instinct and must be governed by insight. Insight is wisdom that discerns the underlying structures of reality (the voice of God). Sexuality is more than biological impulse; to violate the role and function of sexuality releases a marred reality of such force that it consumes. The intensity of harm caused by violating the structures of reality in relation to sexual structures that govern humanity is responsible for immeasurable affects of death in our souls and our societies. To ignore the structure of sin found in both Scripture and reality is to fail at the task of good religious teaching.

Procreation is godlike because our children are born in the likeness and image of God. It is not the act of sexuality that is godlike, it is the birthing and parenting.[4] For the woman this experience is born in pain. For the male it is the responsible knowing that he is the one who has caused pain in the one he loves. Parenting and marriage reflect the relationship of God and humanity. In this sense, sexuality is redeemed through godlike suffering that gives freely of self for the life and blessing of family. Although we are mothers and fathers, we are all children of God.

---

4. Lady wisdom in Proverbs is "brought forth" through an event for God that is like childbirth, so the same word that describes childbirth is used in the translation "brought forth." Suffering is essential for human existence, growth, and development, in order that we might be formed into children of God by insight and choice through God's giving of self, God's Spirit.

## REALITY

This being said, the so-called *fall* narrative is contemplation on the human condition and our journey begins outside the mythical garden of innocence. The myth enables the imagination. Imagination belongs to likeness and image and serves in order that we might seek paradise where humanity and God the creator live in harmony. The Genesis narrative makes a powerful statement in relation to technology. The created environment, though hostile, can only be reconciled to God through the reconciliation of humanity. Our problems with reality are not ultimately outward, but inward.

# Spheres of Existence and Human Reality

### The Aesthetic Weakness

*Pleasing to the eye*
*The sensuous desire for beauty*
*Willing to sacrifice life for appearances—Character for image*
*What is good must be governed*
*Instinct is to be ruled by love*
*Insight reigns when beauty is inwardness of soul*

PART OF BEING HUMAN is to live and exist with some degree of aesthetic desire. This sphere of existence is joined with two others: the ethical and the religious. These three permeate our existence and experience of life. Each sphere is distinct and functions only in relationship with the other two. Whether the relationship is correct or not determines the character of a person. I will begin with Scripture's garden narrative where etiology and foundational teaching on humanity is part of the writer's intent.

The story of Eve's reasoning when moved by desire and prohibited by divine command, portrays her humanity at the tree of the knowledge of good and evil. Her inward thoughts (reason) for consuming the fruit of the forbidden tree are presented by the narrator. These reasons sit in contrast to her response before God when she blames the serpent.[1] As a result, the

---

1. The serpent is an undomesticated beast of the field (it cannot speak). Eve's projection of thought onto the serpent reveals her inward thoughts in relation to doubt. Doubt drives the human intellect and the desire to understand reality. Questions born of doubt can be destructive if not harmonized with ethical thought and faith. Pharaoh's headpiece (crown) bore a serpent and a vulture. The serpent, as a symbol in the ancient Near East, represented power and wisdom. The vulture represented power to bring death—that

# REALITY

Genesis narrative of Eve's moment of decision is portrayed in both mythical and reasoned events; however, reason fails a strict dialectic, reason is limited, myth used wisely appeals to the unknown, the transcendent, the imagination, spirit, even faith in the unseen, i.e., the invisible God.

> *So when the woman saw that the tree was good for food,*
> *and that it was a delight to the eyes,*
> *and that the tree was to be desired to make one wise,*
> *she took of its fruit and ate; and she also gave some to her husband,*
> *who was with her, and he ate.*
> (Gen 3:6)

Initially, Eve recognized that the tree was good for food. Her observational sense is that the prohibition is not ethically justifiable. As she continued to gaze upon the fruit of the forbidden tree her aesthetic sense judged the fruit to be pleasing to the eyes. In the end the tree's endowment of wisdom ignites her religious sense of reality and so she partakes of the fruit and shares the fruit with her nonresistant husband, who has been present throughout her contemplative dialogue. Eve demonstrates intellectual capacity while Adam acts like god watching or is likely complicit and bearing similar thoughts. The Hebrew text is clear that Adam was *with* Eve and use of the word *with* is a literary hint at more than merely being present.

The entire Genesis narrative is finely crafted literature meant to communicate universal truth about humanity and the world we construct. The stories in Genesis, whether from chapters 1—11 or the patriarchal narratives that complete the book, are all more about humanity than they are about God. God is not the major character in Genesis, although he is the constant character; overall humanity revealed in all her need is the driving character of Genesis. The ongoing revelation of God portrayed in Genesis through myth, the lives of the patriarchs, and their wives, is in relation to promises and human failure. Eve's story demonstrates this truth. In Genesis God creates, watches, redeems, makes promises, and is incredibly patient.

The reader is provided with access to Eve's inner thoughts and if the order of Eve's sensing desire is meaningful, it is reasonable to note our first need after breathing is food. The ethics of consumption begins with food and the eye. The poor eat because they are hungry. The rich like pretty food, served up in small, over-priced portions, and always prepared and served

---

is power over life, a power understood to affirm the sovereignty of every state. Rather than develop insight culminating in surrender to faith, Eve's instinctual desire for power marred her reasoning and the relationship of her existential spheres of existence.

by someone else. The ethical must govern the aesthetic. This is so because the aesthetic engages our sense of beauty and order; left alone, the aesthetic ignores the ethical.

The ethical and the aesthetic are both to be governed by the religious; which is the pursuit of wisdom because God revealed is wisdom.

> *...Christ the power of God and the wisdom of God.*
> *1 Cor 1:24b*

Eve represents the survival instinct that sacrifices good for evil and ignores wisdom's prohibition. The tree was identified as the tree of the knowledge of good and evil. The prohibition set it apart as unlike all other trees only in relation to the prohibition. This, in Eve's view (for she represents humanity and is also *Adamah*), is the point of denial, signifying that she (and Adam with her) are not accepting of limits they do not understand. Yet the existential damage to her own being is caused because she did not recognize the religious as a relational reality and not merely prohibition. Reaching beyond the structures of reality, sacrificing God, others, and the creation become the inheritance of Eve's children; it is the world God has created and the reality humanity continues to create.

Faith belongs to the sphere of the religious. Faith is the corrective to Eve's errant reasoning. Faith enables humanity to live with creaturely limits while bearing the image of God allows our insight to identify the limits of humanity's domination over creation as prohibition.

## THE AESTHETIC PERSONALITY

The relationship of the aesthetic personality with the ethical and the religious is transient and sporadic. To order the world and enjoy the beauty of creation is, in part, to be like God. To be creative and produce music, works of art, fine literature, poetic philosophy, to design clothing, and produce beauty in the world we live in, all these are good. However, when love for aesthetics is the dominant trait of a human being's personality or governs their view of people, society, culture, and life, then that person will be unstable in relation to goodness and fail at the river of justice. They will sacrifice for the sake of self-determined order and resist the perceived chaos of difference that belongs to humanity (our differences are God's will).

An aesthetic personality is a shallow person who views people based upon their appearance. The aesthetic personality does not recognize the subjectivity of aesthetic judgments. The association of the aesthetic with goodness will lead to mistaking appearances for morality. This failure in a highly structured society will blind an aesthetic culture or politic. In this environment the ones who are considered—in spite of obvious moral failure—to be moral, to be righteous, are those who succeed, those who conform, and those who have wealth, power, and influence.

## LOVE AND COMFORT IN RELATION TO THE AESTHETIC

Because all human beings function within the three spheres of existence, each of us is prone to allow love for the aesthetic to capsize our better senses. For this reason it is important not to love the aesthetic, but to appreciate beauty as a morally ambiguous reality that must be subjected to the ethical. An aesthetic person, without the ethical, is a vehicle for the entrance of evil into the world.[2] A spiritually intelligent person will feel discomfort when the word "love" is used to speak about beauty. Love belongs to the realm of the living, the breathing—of humanity that bears the image of God. God is love and love must have an object; only living beings can be objects for love because only living beings can return love.

In any nation where ordered environments display wealth and power while lack of essentials for living plagues the populace, then the aesthetic is a systemic evil that represents a manicured world. This kind of environment is produced at the cost of moral judgments in economic relationships; it is the illusion of Disneyland. In an aesthetic culture the value of a human being is often judged based upon their car, their home, and the maintenance of their lawn. Order at the cost of a functioning moral conscience is dehumanizing.

The aesthetic is a comforting power because of the perception of beauty we attribute to our particular tastes for artistic expression. Once the pride of the aesthetic overtakes the ethical then wealth or money begins to define the aesthetic. It is at this point when the wealthy spend enormous amounts of money on a piece of art that is little more than arbitrarily splattered paint on a canvas. Pride and the aesthetic, mixed with power, results in absurdity.

---

2. The manifestation of the aesthete with power is often displayed in love for architecture. The messiness of living is not present in costly architectural extravagance; it is like a picture of a city without people.

The real beauty of the aesthetic is its simplicity, its humanity, its ability to touch the heart and produce love and compassion; of course this response is dependent upon the receptive heart. I was walking amongst the shanties of desperately poor families living outside a small landfill where they scavenged to survive. As I passed along in front of one of the homes I was moved by the presence of the comfort of the aesthetic. Living in severe conditions of oppressive neglect one family had used some paint remaining in a discarded can to paint flowers on the front of their home that was constructed with discarded pieces of wood. To the left of the front entrance (an opening with a hanging piece of linen) placed atop a few flat rocks was a couple of broken pots each with a planting of vegetation. The comforting display of the aesthetic in its simplicity is a very human act. In an environment of stench, flies, filth, and hunger, this little act of artistic beauty brought tears to my eyes.

## THE AESTHETE AND SOCIAL COHESION

Social cohesion at the sacrifice of truth is often mistaken for social intelligence. This is so because it is embodied in a personality. The life of an intelligent aesthete is often marked by success. In a world where being spiritually intelligent requires speech that identifies sociocultural dysfunction, the intelligent aesthete chooses the comfort of accommodation for the sake of social cohesion. The intelligent aesthete refuses truth and will not engage in criticism of the established order. In religious communities, the life of these persons expresses the unethical values of the larger society as congruent with the faith. In relation to the ethical, their lives masquerade the ethical as the approved order of sociocultural politics. They are good citizens, good people, they are happy, they smile, they are mimetic models for the simple and exemplars for the dominant powers of wealth and success. They are concerned with their image more than their character.

At the core of the aesthetic personality is the violence of sacrificial progress. An aesthetic personality, regardless of faith claims, is, in practice, a social Darwinist.[3] In his/her world, merciful justice is lost to penal sacrifice of any who challenge the status quo. These persons abandon intellectual thought for legal reasoning that is without the Spirit of Christ. This

---

3. Adolf Hitler's use of aesthetics as a propaganda tool that functioned via culture is an example of how an aesthetic personality void of ethics and religion is a person without conscience. There are numerous books on this subject.

is so because they are not subjected to ethical thought but dominated by their aesthetic-centered personality.

These souls do not understand the transformative power of the reign of God, they believe in sacrificial progress. Their ability to ignore the poor while smiling is reflective of a spiritual illness. An aesthete ignores the goodness in humanism but embraces the religious as the deification of a sacrificial order—religion's weakness is its use of the aesthetic in place of a lived practice that meets the morality of Jesus. The aesthete is afraid of the disorder involved in transformative change, but tolerates social injustice and identifies the normalization of war as representative of a healthy patriotism. They do not understand that Jesus is Lord of the chaos. They avoid any form of prophetic denunciation because their religion is cheap grace served up sweet for the blind.

## THE AESTHETIC CULTURE

The aesthetic culture is spiritless. It is a materialistic culture where the value of a human being is based upon worth signified by accumulation. Global capitalism is the purveyor of this dehumanizing drive that functions on instinct rather than compassion, rather than humanness.

In an aesthetic culture aging is a curse to be resisted with extreme measures of self-preservation. The gradual result is that the wisdom and influence of aged persons without wealth is lost because they do not display the aesthetic expectation of youthful appearance. Without the storytelling of the aged who are able to connect younger persons with a living history, the development of a generation of ahistorical persons who think of themselves as the center of existence is birthed.

The impact of the advent, or invasion, of wireless communications as normative for the human experience is still unfolding. Its potential for good is real, yet its potential for increased accumulation and evil is amplified by mobility for the wealthy or at least citizens of wealthy nations. This is so because the disparity of wealth and power between people groups leads to the exploitation of the economically deprived.

This eruption of technological advance has produced the naturally disruptive reality of the younger generation teaching the older generation. Older persons have lived without technology's claim upon human happiness. Younger persons accept technology without thought, while older persons are more apathetic. Technology's permeating presence into all aspects of life eventually intrudes deeply enough that older persons must accept its role in life. So the younger teach the older and this has contributed to an ahistorical generation. The technologically adept younger generation loses their sense of history because they have become teachers of their elders.

This phenomenon of an ahistorical generation is supported by the relationship of technology and social Darwinism. In such an environment the concept of progress is supported by technology rather than ethics. In this environment the remaking or redefining of humanity is tested through behaviors which were previously considered aberrant. The ahistorical culture is like all millennial expectations; it celebrates a chance to *start over*, free from the past.

An aesthetic culture lacks the ethics to halt the landslide effect of materialist idolatry and the pursuit of eternal youth. The result is historical violence; meaning not only is history set aside in the attempt to *start over*, but the ensuing violence caused by redefining humanity is historical; it will fail, it will be assigned to the annals of history.

Aesthetic influence on a culture separated from ethics and religion, or as the dominant influence, is the most demonic form of culture. The aesthetic culture courts the demonic because it replaces what is *good* with cultural judgments on what constitutes beauty. In an aesthetic culture, the flourishing of life is replaced by efforts at longevity and comfort. In an aesthetic culture, people use birth control in an unhealthy way and limit children to one or none.

The aesthetic sphere is the weakest of the three. This is so because the aesthetic is the least dependent upon insight and gravitates toward culturally engrained instincts that direct perspectives on what constitutes beauty. The ethical leads to the writing of legislation in society. The ethical is to pursue the preservation of life in relation to one another. The religious inculcates concepts of wisdom related to the finer attributes of being human.

When the aesthetic dominates a culture it pushes the culture toward instinct and voids intellect. So the redefining of humanity free from history's lessons erupts in idolatry of the human. I mean the pursuit of wisdom as the search for God in the creation is lost to experimentation that the physical world resists. Longevity, violent birth control (e.g., abortion and insufficient number of children to constitute replacement or multiplication), and homosexuality mark the presence of an aesthetic culture.

REALITY

## IDOLATRY OF THE HUMAN

The aesthetic culture culminates in violence built on idolatry of the human, by exploiting human freedom to form reality. It is a freedom that rejects all constraint from historical ethics or religious claims on reality. Idolatry of the human is a sign that religion has failed. Populous religion caters to the idolatry of the human and love for aesthetics, for longevity, for comfort, for abandoning history, it ends thought and ends life. The idolatry of the human always leads to nationalism, simply because for aesthetics to function, some people must be less human.

Longevity, as an ultimate concern placed firmly in the center of culture, results in a society where death is no longer natural, no longer a gift at the end of a full life and an aged body. Inevitably, longevity as an ultimate concern inhibits the maturation of wisdom in the elderly; religion teaches us how to die (*ars moriendi*).[4]

> *And deliver them who through fear of death were all their lifetime subject to bondage. (Heb 2:15)*

The pursuit of wealth is essential for longevity and hopes to maintain the appearance of youthfulness. A life in pursuit of longevity, with an identity formed around appearances and built on wealth, results in greed that holds back the resources of life for children. Wealthy populations do not increase in number through procreative living. The sexual impulse is strong and fulfills the poor's need for a little pleasure and God's desire for us to fill the earth.

> *He said to his people, "Look, the Israelite people are more numerous and more powerful than we."*
> *Exod 1:9*

In the end the aesthetic corrupts humanity until self-destructiveness turns toward the most instinctual behavior, specifically sexual behavior. The abuse of women is validated through conquering armies. A people are not conquered until the female gender is sexually dominated by systemic structures of exploitation. It was not until 1945 that marriage of a US soldier to an Asian woman was legalized. Thousands of children born to US

---

4. The illegal purchasing of human organs that flourishes in poor countries is an example of the conflicting realities of life and death with wealth and poverty. The pursuit of youth is the pursuit of longevity. *Ars moriendi* is Latin for "the art of dying," and is a literary work belonging to the Christian tradition.

soldiers in Vietnam were not allowed entry into the US until 1989. To this day the children of US soldiers born to Filipina women are not granted entry to the US.[5] Across Asia, in Korea, Thailand, Vietnam, Japan, and the Philippines, US soldiers left behind their children.

The aesthetic idolatry of the human exploits sexuality until the culture, its language, and every facet of life is sexualized. Without restraint, sexual behavior descends into violence. In the end homosexuality and gender confusion are normalized under the idea of love for humanity. It is the end of life; a world without ethics, a world without wisdom. The establishment of an aesthetic culture marks the end of a civilization.

---

5. Johnson, *Mixed Race America*. The estimated number of children left behind (as were their mothers) by US soldiers upon their withdrawal in 1992 is 50,000 (see Moon, *Sex Among Allies*, 35.

# Chaos and the Human Condition

### Monsters

*Unexplainable feelings of fear*
*Uncertainty, where is it from?*
*I've tried so hard*
*It all comes undone*
*Alone I face monsters*
*Where has everyone gone?*
*Together they've slain us*
*Will we rise?*
*Jesus is with me*
*Doing nothing?*
*Still he is with me*
*I charged the darkness*
*Like a knight of faith*
*Solitary, naked, unarmed*
*Still he is with me*
*Will daylight come?*
*It has been dark for so long.*
*I am undone*
*Has the monster won?*

THE DAILY EXPERIENCE OF living that gives rise to *monsters* is a constant and will remain a common predictable event until the *telos*. The possibility for the eruption of monsters (Leviathan) is always just below the surface. The rising of the monster is brought about by the tension present in human relationships. This is so whether it is merely a couple of brothers or in larger relational formations such as the cultural, national, and international. The continual collision of chaos in life is a reckoning of hidden failure, misunderstanding, and evil covered over by false civility and niceness. It is the tension brought on simply by existing, a tension that permeates each life, every society, the entire world.

In its immanence, the rise of Leviathan is a product of the perennial idols (militarism, materialism, and ethnocentrism). In the present era the monster is the unsustainable consumption of the world's resources by the wealthy, the powerful, and in particular the US Hyper Power. Within the boundaries of the US the cost of rising to the status of a hyper power has required a cultural ethos built around the sacralizing of warriors and the development of a warrior culture. Christendom (popular evangelicalism) in the US has embraced the warrior culture and, in doing so, has lost what it means to be a Christian.[1]

We are creatures in process, for us becoming is before being. It is religion that endeavors to aid people in a transformative life of becoming, of changing. All our becoming is lived out witin the presence of monsters, that is, powers beyond our control who, like parasites, draw the life out of us, causing the closest of relationships to suffer their murderous interruptions.

## ON MONSTERS

I was conversing with my daughter about the terminal illness of her mother and did not think my eight-year-old granddaughter playing behind us was listening. It was my birthday so we enjoyed blowing out candles and eating a piece of cake. Suddenly my granddaughter began to cry with deep emotion. I asked why she was crying. She began an elaborate story about her fear of a doll coming to life and bearing a knife and seeking to kill people.

My thoughts were that she had heard our conversation; unable to comprehend the reality of death and dying she needed a monster. She knew the monster she created wasn't real, but her feelings needed an explanation she was incapable of expressing. We all live with this reality of the nearness of some monstrous force threatening the well being of our lives. Apocalyptic

---

1. Plato's philosophy of a warrior class permeates evangelical thought. The invitation of military officers to speak in churches to celebrate Veterans" Day and Memorial Day has contributed to the unquestioned acceptance of Plato's thought. Plato's thought has been used to indoctrinate generations of military and political leaders beginning in prep schools for the wealthy, e.g., Montgomery Bell Academy in Nashville.

literature fulfills a role in Scripture that addresses the birth of monsters, both real and imagined. Behind every monster is fear, misunderstanding, tragedy, natural disaster, or human conflict. History's monsters are always larger than the men who nurture them.

## NAMING LEVIATHAN'S CHILDREN

Racism is the deep-seated ignorance of an undercurrent in all American social reality that supports and feeds the monster of white superiority. The biblicism that did not understand the book of Joshua as a conquest narrative, as a piece of literature, contributed to the co-opting of God for the service of war and genocide as western Europeans arrived in America. Scripture became a tool for justifying the state rather than instructive on the human propensity to war in the name of God.

Good theology serves as a corrective guide to the ever-present push from culture and government to reign over humanity. When theology serves to justify state killing and cultural injustice, then religion becomes useless for transformation and serves the idols of the age. The monster of racism exists in the presence of white superiority built into American history and appears in colloquialisms, books, movies, and perceptions of what constitutes beauty.

Wealth disparity exhibited in abject poverty is a monster. To end the injustices of limitless wealth and extreme poverty lies at the heart of the Torah, it echoes throughout the prophets and is the activity that follows acceptance of the gospel; it is the activity that begins the healing of the world. The need for correcting the illegal accumulation of wealth through injustice, through legalized crimes in the halls of power, is pressing humanity and will not end without a response.

Christian leaders and theologians should be the first responders speaking denunciation to the injustice of current economic systems, and directors of nonviolent resistance by the people. Our world needs saner voices than the keepers of the status quo. The words "Remember the poor" should endlessly echo in the heart and mind of every Christian.

Of course there are many monsters to be named. The complexity in personal relationships that gives rise to monsters is as complicated as the few I have named in relation to larger systems of states, cultures, and social stratifications.

In personal relationships, particularly familial, the tension of the unspoken and the buildup of careless words produce an uncontainable monster that will disrupt the relationship if equality and love are not nurtured, if forgiveness is not given. People who love each other often cannot have a healthy relationship because one or both of them do not address their own failures. Claims of absolute innocence in personal relationships are always false; we are all guilty. Arrogance, pride, controlling words, and hurtful words all float around in the atmosphere of human relationships like a disease in the body.

## LIVING WITH MONSTERS

It is notable that theology has often ignored the first creation account's assertion that God created the *great sea monsters* or serpents or dragons—all are legitimate translations—and called them good. It is significant that of the seven times the word *create* is used in Genesis 1–2:4a, one of the uses is applied to the creation of mythical creatures that represent chaos.

> So God created the great sea monsters and every living creature
> that moves,
> of every kind, with which the waters swarm, and every winged bird
> of every kind. And God saw that it was good.
> (Gen 1:21)

The chaos motif is firmly rooted in the OT and particularly in the Genesis account. Although the first Genesis account serves as a polemic in relation to the Babylonian creation myth *Enuma Elish*, it also displays the role of humanity in relation to creation as one of domination, not servitude to cosmic gods. The second account shifts to validate the distinctive value of humanity as image-bearing vice-regents caring for and naming God's creation. Humanity is loved of God and capable of naming the creation. Humanity is responsible for building their reality as image-bearing creatures. However they must do so while living with forces beyond their control. Theology is required to view the existence of chaos in reality as essential for the purposes of God in relation to humanity.

We are not ready for heaven, nor are we fit for utopia. Rather, we are creatures in process, moving from a beginning to an end, a birth to a death. We might view chaos as the absence of God in creation and human reality. It is good that chaos is present in a creation in which God withholds his nature (holiness). God is not *in creation* and although the creation exists within God, it exists as work, witness and home for humanity.

Humanity is *up from the ground* belonging to the material from which creation is made of. Humanity is the hope of God and the reason for sustaining the creation with his will. Our journey in the land of monsters is at the heart of human experience.[2] We are not in control of reality, regardless of all our efforts, the underlying current of invisible tensions will rise like a raging dragon. Scripture counsels us that (unlimited) forgiveness for the repentant, along with love and understanding, enable us to live through the dark night of poisonous serpents.

Tragedy, catastrophe, and unexplainable evil in myriad manifestations capture every human being's life. Learning to survive the monsters is a formidable challenge when faith cannot subdue trials of darkness. How we survive these dark moments is what makes us who we are. When reason has vanished, confusion reigns, when God cannot be found, we must remember that Jesus suffers alongside us; suffering is essential for character formation.

> *And not only that, but we also boast in our sufferings,*
> *knowing that suffering produces endurance,*
> *and endurance produces character,*
> *and character produces hope,*
> *(Rom 5:3-4)*

It should be every believer's desire for the igniting of the human imagination, with hope and faith, to enable each one of us so that we live out the in-breaking of the reign of God with the belief that change in humanity is possible. However, all these efforts are accomplished without the benefit of the imagined change. The Christian life is lived out as a star on a dark night with no one to see its glory. Love must suffer the mess of living and lay aside any idea of being acquitted for personal culpability in the conflicts of relationships.

In personal relationships, chasing monsters—that is, looking for cause and blame—is our normal practice, but is an insufficient practice. Life is far too complicated and the origin of monsters beyond our capacity to dissect. Rather, humility, forgiving speech, and refusing to let the monster win must

---

2. Rene Girard's theory of violence as a contagion built upon desire and mimetic behavior addresses the monster as a parasitical tension in the reality of relationships on every level. The monster is a parasitical beast who doesn't know forgiveness.

be our *ultimate concern,* only these will bring reconciliation. Of course we personify our monsters, much like my little granddaughter.

## INTERNATIONAL MONSTERS

In international affairs the failure to recognize the human condition (subject to chaos) in light of uncontrollable underlying tensions results in catastrophic events of war. The personification of the monster is the demonization of the other—that is the competing nation-state as *enemy.* In relation to our capitalist democracy, most often, enemy states are merely those that resist the effort of the other state to acquire more than they give in return. This alone moves one state to resist the ideology of another and adopt an ideology that must be demonized. Becoming human is lived out in the presence of monsters.

Imagine a person who refuses to work even a janitor's job at a nuclear missile facility. I tend to believe there have been some unnamed persons who of good conscience have rejected such employment. Unfortunately most persons are so captured in the madness that we have lost the inner fortitude and courage to resist and call others to resistance. That the Christian church does not address very practical issues of moral living compromised by the power of institutional normalization is a disservice to both God and humanity. The immorality, the crime against both God and humanity existent in building a nuclear arsenal, is the most life-threatening reality ever devised by any group of people. It is the monster of self-destruction. Like the shadow of death it looms over us all—this ominous power that so many do not believe will ever be used. Nuclear weapons are not an impotent deterrent, they are kept launch-ready so that they can be used.

# CATEGORY IV

# SEX AND ROMANTIC LOVE

# Sex, Violence, Sin, and Death

## The Coward

*Where's that bastard death?*
*Let's put an end to his terror!*
*Rip out his lungs and feed his heart to dragons.*
*Only a poet can personify an impersonal reality.*
*Only a priest can claim a little god under the almighty God.*
*There is only one God and one Lord Jesus Christ.*
*When will this terror end?*
*In my soul I'm alive and resist the bastard.*
*While he kills me I mock him with my will*
*Sour, bitter—useless unwinding of life*
*or*
*Catastrophic, immediate horror—a quick end*
*or*
*Lingering, malicious, inhumane—living death*
*Where is God?*
*In between or beyond?*
*Death as judgment*
*Death as enemy*
*Are we all so wretched?*
*Do we all deserve to die?*
*This affront to life*
*This that devalues the apex of God's work*
*I will not be silent*
*O God we could use a little more help*

# SEX AND ROMANTIC LOVE

*Be near and not far*
*For at my death I will curse death—your judgment*
*and*
*Impale your enemy with my embrace of life*
*I will overcome with Christ Jesus my King*

## SEX AND SIN ENTER THE WORLD

*Death insists that life is real*
*Only a creature created for eternity views death as an unacceptable reality.*
*Death devalues life but the image of God in us empowers us to overcome*
*and value life with self-giving acts of love. The resurrection is the deification*
*of humanity as creature, to be the beloved children of God*

Sex and sin enter the world at the same time as death. I understand that the sexual impulse is instinctual. Animals have instinct. We have insight. Our primary instinct is the sexual impulse.[1]

Jesus' words teach that marriage is not a part of the resurrection experience (Matt 22:30). Understanding marriage as the covenantal relationship for assuring procreation and family, then both these realities must change and sexuality ceases. I think if the instinct or impulse to sexuality is removed we will not miss it—memory fades over time. However I think gender must play some ongoing role in the resurrection. He created us male and female and this was pronounced good, so gender will be preserved. It is part of our identity and cannot be lost in resurrection. I also understand why the Johannine Epistles say that our resurrected reality is not yet fully conceivable; there are many unanswerable questions.

I think history exists specifically because of the presence of death. Death and violence cannot be separated because the entrance of death was brought by an existential act of violence as humanity rejected the voice of God. Without death or violence, history has no relevance in existence.

---

1. Sexuality is instinctual because we do not need to be taught it. Flight or fight is not an instinct but a response to fear. Fear in a human being is subject to rational thought and not merely instinctual, even if it is based upon superstition. Other aspects of human behavior like anger and jealousy are emotions and expressive of limitations, weaknesses, and relational challenges; they are mimetic, and can be overcome rationally. The sexual impulse is not mere emotion; it is part of our biology. The sexual instinct exists in our body and it touches the mind with its power.

## Sex, Violence, Sin, and Death

This is why God is without a history until creation begins. In the Eden story, sex, violence, sin, and death all enter the world at the same moment. Without humanity there is no procreation, violence, sin, death, or history. God cannot reveal God's self apart from history or apart from the existence of image-bearing creatures. The history of God begins with the emergent consciousness of humanity outside the mythic garden. Any events prior to humanity's consciousness are mythical.[2]

That human beings have a beginning, enter the world as limited creatures with unlimited imagination, is indicative of both finite reality and infinite possibility. So enters our conflict with death and its inevitability in relation to our existence. Created in the image of God we are, in a sense, deity in conflict (Ps 82:6; John 10:34).

God had to enter into history to reveal God's self and provide humanity with a relational connection to God if humanity was to experience life beyond death.[3] God can only reveal God's self to image-bearing creatures within a construct where procreation, violence, sin, and death exist in history. This is so because God is a creating, nonviolent, holy, redemptive being of love longing for a family.

The theme of God being able to create human beings apart from our participation is demonstrated in the reversal of menopause in Sarah and infertility in Abraham (his body referred to as dead). The virgin birth likewise attests to God not needing males in order to bring human beings into the world. Of course the creation of Adam and Eve also makes the birthing of life a divine fiat independent of human participation. I like teaching young men how important it is to value their power to participate in the creation of human beings with God and their wife. Our fragility as males is front and center to remind us not to use our strength for violence but to protect the possibility for life existent in our loins.

In the concept of the virgin birth is both the activity of God and humanity. It is the first movement toward God reclaiming the power to create life as distinctly God's alone. Further, as I have stressed, a beginning for image-bearing creatures requires a history, a beginning inevitably includes death, and God can only reveal God's self to his creatures within a historical

---

2. Prehistoric creatures are void of a history; their existence is inconsequential as creatures without insight, without a consciousness of becoming or understanding of violence, sin, and death.

3. Finiteness requires limits, an end; only an infinite being (God) is limitless. God alone is infinite, is life, and only that which is incorporated into God can enjoy eternal life. Christ Jesus, the son of man (human being), conquered death.

construct where death exists. For this reason God is a redeeming being and God must work to have a family. The apex of God's creation is humanity; the pinnacle of God's work to reveal God's self is the life, death, and resurrection of Jesus.

# God's Heart for Sexually Exploited Persons

### A Single Mom

*She weeps*
*He hides*
*She bears a child*
*He hides*
*She is shamed*
*He is a man*
*She raises a son alone*
*He is a better man than his father*

GOD CLOSES HIS EYES to our constructions of personal sin when systemic structures of evil prevail and cause the weak, the poor, and children to become victims of an unhealthy society. The definition of a victim is that they are innocent. The attribution of sin to a victim is an ignorant, self-righteous rant of religious absurdity. The inheritance of sin is not through genetic relationship; it is the resulting relation of all humanity through societal constructs of power that corrupt reality.

*The status of a woman as a prostitute is indicative of systemic sin in society, and governing males are guilty of sin more than any sins women will be held accountable of before God.*[1]

---

1. The italicized statement is supported by a God speech, written in poetry by the prophet Hosea (Hos 4:14). It is affirming of my claim that men are held accountable for the sexual behavior of women in society.

# SEX AND ROMANTIC LOVE

## SCAPEGOATING A WOMAN AND RELIGIOUS VIOLENCE

### John 8:1–10

The biblical portrayals of Jesus compassion for sexually exploited women communicate his understanding of their status as victims. The story of the woman caught in adultery and the incredulous behavior of those who seek to stone her is an example of Jesus' sensitivity to evil. The male perpetrator of this sin is not present and the woman is a victim of a plot by the Pharisees who are more interested in building a case against Jesus than the woman's alleged violation of Moses' law. The woman is said to be guilty of adultery, even caught in the act.

Jesus certainly knows the law so his response is ultimately instructive on how to read and understand the passages of the law that call for killing. The constant refrain to put people to death is to communicate how damaging certain human behavior is to life. Moses' extreme call for stoning is a literary deterrent; it is impractical for society and inconsistent with God's mercy. It is instructive on the power of sin to bring death into the world.

Jesus' response indicates that the Pharisees do not possess anything written by the hand of God. So the Lord bends down to write in the sand, a rather nonchalant if not disruptive response from a teacher, from a man being confronted by persons of power with the intent to include him along with the woman as victims of a frenzied stoning. Our imaginations are left to wonder what Jesus (with the finger of God) wrote in the dirt. Initially it is the act of a child to play in the dirt, a simple mannerism that reveals Jesus' practice; he writes nothing, rather, he lives. Perhaps he wrote out all the reasons for stoning presented in the law? The teaching would have been profound for who would not be guilty? The wages of sin are death. We do not need to kill anyone; we are already dying.

When their questioning continued, Jesus made an upward movement and invited any who would accuse the woman to throw the first stone. Public acts of violence always need someone to throw the first stone. Jesus knew the reality of the moment, if a stone was thrown, the stone-thrower would be exposed as a killer. The absence of the male adulterer is too conspicuous to be ignored; the male must be stoned also according to Moses. The Pharisees knew this and could not respond to Jesus' challenge for a first stone.

Jesus returns to writing in the dirt, the departure of the group begins with the oldest and one by one all the accusers leave. In the story we are left with only Jesus and the woman. The Pharisees are faced with this truth:

the Decalogue says do not kill as well as do not commit adultery, and yet they sought to kill Jesus, an innocent man. This is so because it is evident that if the stoning of the woman began it would be built upon Jesus defying the law and they would see to the death of both Jesus and the woman. The crowd would ignite in unleashed violence and the Pharisees could deny their complicity in any purposeful scheme set on stoning Jesus. Jesus hit the weakness of their plan: one of them, one of the Pharisees, would have to throw the first stone because they were the accusers.

The Law of Moses had met its authoritative interpreter. The religious had the murder in their hearts exposed, their claim as interpreters of Moses challenged, and the scapegoating of the woman made clear by the actions of Jesus. Jesus would not leave the woman whom they had stood before him. Jesus' insight into the plan of the Pharisees is matched by Jesus' wisdom of the Torah. In effect, Jesus has abolished the death penalty. There is murder in the hearts of the most religious among us.

The wedding motif is prevalent throughout the gospel of John. In our story, the woman represents the body of Christ; there is no condemnation. Likewise, we are invited to view a picture of Jesus kneeling before a woman as a man does before his beloved. Jesus defends the woman who was merely a scapegoat for the Pharisees. John's gospel in this story communicates that all are guilty of the adultery of idolatry. In the case of the Pharisees, their idolatry was to believe they were the interpreters of the law and had the power to murder both the woman and Jesus in a scheme of violent deception. The power over life belongs to God and God alone. The state and religion's claims upon the right to take life are incompatible with the reign of God entering the world marked by Jesus' entrance into history.

## THE BURDEN OF BEAUTY

## John 4

I am going to take a perspective on the woman at the well that is a reasonable assertion based upon the story though not stated explicitly. I am also not presenting the many wonderful readings available to the interpreter from this rich and meaningful story. So, I will argue for and read the story through a lens that understands the (nameless) woman at the well to be representative of women whose burden is their beauty.

# SEX AND ROMANTIC LOVE

First, the invitation of the Samaritan woman to the people of the city informs the reader that the conversation of the nameless woman and Jesus was longer than the crafted literature we receive in the text.

> "Come and see a man who told me everything I have ever done! He cannot be the Messiah, can he?"
> (John 4:29)

I do not understand her words to be exaggeration but to be an accurate statement on her encounter with Jesus. Our view into their conversation is limited to the defining events of her identity in the eyes of others. A woman who goes through four husbands and serves as a mistress to another man cannot conceal or keep this part of her life from defining her when other people speak about her. The absence of any mention of children, and her presence at the well alone is compatible with the idea that her relationships were dependent upon sustaining her beauty.[2]

The woman does not represent all Samaritans, although her namelessness does allow her to represent the body of Christ because of the wedding motif in John. Women are often left nameless to communicate how males treat them. At other times leaving a character nameless is a literary device to indicate that the character represents an entire group of people. However, I think the nameless Samaritan woman represents both the bride of Christ and all women who are loved only for their beauty. This is consistent with the ease in which she moves from one husband to another and eventually to a man who is not her husband and so she becomes a mistress to a rich man.

The nameless woman at the well met a man (Jesus) who witnessed the marks of five different men upon a lonely woman whose beauty separated her from other women and made her the preoccupation of men. Alone, she came to the well to draw water in the heat of the day. Ostracized from other women, she had become a plaything for men. I imagine Jesus told her

---

2. The story of Hannah suggests Elkanah sought to preserve Hannah's beauty while obtaining offspring through Penninah; this is observed in Elkanah's response to Hannah's desire for children. Elkanah's lack of empathy is in his statement that he is more fulfilling to Hannah than ten sons. Providing her with a double portion as sacrifice to the LORD is said to be his expression of love. In the OT, wombs are opened and closed by the LORD. This statement is more a theological affirmation of the LORD as the source of life than an accurate rendering of events. Efforts at birth control through withdrawal or other means was culturally and religiously unacceptable; however, that males chose otherwise in order to preserve the beauty of a favored wife is compatible with the behavior of males in the OT and throughout history. The stories of Adah (ornament) and Zillah (shadow) in Genesis affirm the concept of a favored wife through the meaning of their names.

things about herself that she kept from all others. He saw into her heart and saw her dreams. Jesus saw past her beauty and reached her soul with truth.

## THE FORGIVEN ESCORT OF FAITH

### Luke 7:36–50

All four gospels record a story about the anointing of Jesus' feet. Luke's is my favorite; it is an encounter involving Jesus, a high-class escort, and a judgmental Pharisee. It is clear that Jesus had some impact upon the nameless woman and that she also knew Simon the Pharisee. In an environment where men can commit adultery and not be held accountable, it is possible that her knowledge of Simon might be more than traditional readings have offered. She does know his name and where he lives.

The nameless woman identified by Simon the Pharisee as a sinner hears that Jesus is to eat at Simon's home. She immediately takes with her the tools of her trade, costly scented oil. Upon her arrival at the home of Simon she manages to make her way inside. I can imagine people moving out of the way for her simply because she would have been considered an unseemly character who good people avoided.

Once inside she sees Jesus and a quick glance affirms her thoughts; Simon has not received Jesus into his home with dignity, he has not provided water for his feet, his head has not been touched with oil. Jesus is seated on the pillows at the low table, he is positioned on the side of his hip, his feet are behind him and he leans on his left hand. She begins to weep; this man named Jesus has touched her life and shown grace like no other (man) religious teacher. She lets her hair down and takes shame upon herself for doing so, her tears flow so heavy that she uses them to wash Jesus' feet. Her very long hair becomes a towel for the feet of the itinerant teacher. Then the room fills with the costly scent identified with a woman of the night as she oils Jesus' feet.

We are told Simon's thoughts but they should not be surprising. We've learned enough already to know how a man like Simon thinks. It is questionable as to who would be forgiven much if Simon were to recognize his own need of Jesus. We know Jesus intends to forgive the woman. Her actions indicate her love for Jesus, for his teaching, and her repentance. Jesus rebukes Simon for his display of inhospitable treatment. The woman has reversed all of Simon's social snubs directed at Jesus.

Jesus publicly and in a personal address announces that the woman's sins are forgiven; obversely, Simon's are not. Jesus follows up his ministry to the woman by informing her that it is her faith that has saved her. Her faith was demonstrated in her actions to resist Simon and honor Jesus.

When she poured out her perfume onto the feet of Jesus it was a symbol of her transformation. She would need the pleasantly odorous oil no longer. This act was the culminating event of all her behavior and confirmed her conversion to the teachings of Jesus.

## ENDANGERED GUARDIANS

Women are the guardians of life. They hold the next generation in their bodies and nurture them with their bodies. In the presence of violence, even a military firefight, women will run into the middle of live fire in order to scoop up the children and get them to safety.

Male children need the influence of women in order to become healthy human beings. Manoah (Samson's father) approaches life from the perspective that males are to be in charge of life and interrupts the influence of Samson's mother with her son. In Manoah's thought, women are not suited to raise male children. This results in the overmasculinization of Samson, who becomes a womanizing fool. The image of the macho male is mocked through the failed life of Samson.

Hannah rears one of Israel's greatest prophets and does so by removing Samuel from the home of his father. She then forms his identity and nurtures his religious life beyond the failed father and priest Eli, who receives Samuel because of the gifts Hannah is able to provide through the wealth of her husband. Women can rear excellent male children without a male.

Males are responsible to produce social structures that ensure the world is a safe place for women to bear and rear children. A world where males are taught war and violence is not a safe place for anyone. Hosea's word in a God speech places responsibility for female sexual behavior upon males:

> *I will not punish your daughters when they play the whore,*
> *nor your daughters-in-law when they commit adultery;*
> *for the men themselves go aside with whores,*
> *and sacrifice with temple prostitutes;*
> *thus a people without understanding comes to ruin.*
> *(Hos 4:14)*

In Hosea, the inebriation of a people lost to idolatry, a people who seek the favor of empire's wealth, who trust in warfare, who make the world a place where ethics and religion are overcome by love for aesthetics, are a people without understanding on how society is to be structured:

> *Assyria shall not save us;*
> *we will not ride upon horses;*
> *we will say no more, "Our God,"*
> *to the work of our hands.*
> *In you the orphan finds mercy.*
> *(Hos 14:3)*

Hosea provides a prayer for Israel in the final hope piece (ch. 14) at the end of his book. The prayer provides for the removal of idols that separate Israel from God and to bring change to a society where male/female relationships have collapsed into the exploitation and abuse of women. The wealth of Assyria cannot rescue them from the famine upon their land (materialism). The chariots of war cannot save them from their enemies (militarism). Their idolatry of the human, their love of self (culminating in unrestrained sexual behavior) is a false god. Israel is orphaned, their God has left them, they ask for mercy.

*Hope pieces are not idealistic dreams of an age to come; rather they are indicative of practice for God's people.*

Endangered guardians are women whose lives have not been properly cared for by males who are responsible before God to produce societies of peace without the presence of idols. When males are not responsible before God for their sexuality, for their seed, then the guardians of life (women) are endangered.

The conquering of a people through military force always includes the sexual conquering of the women. This activity of abusing the guardians of life results in a world inebriated on idols and unable to find their way in the world. When men do not restrain their sexuality as a spiritual discipline, and when women are abused, the world collapses into violence. Women are not prostitutes, they are endangered guardians. The fault for the presence of prostitution is placed upon the males in Scripture, not the women.

I will provide a story to explain how systemic structures produce evil in society, because I don't think most persons even understand the concept of systemic structures of evil. I have seen the following scenarios many times and always to my dismay and tears. A young, uneducated woman suffers debilitating poverty brought on by structural adjustment programs. The young woman is a Christian and out of desperation seeks employment through an agency that promises her a job far from home.

Her home is a place where she is forced to live by scavenging for food and cans and bottles. She lives in an odorous dumpsite in sweltering heat. She accepts the employment offering and is trafficked into bars where US soldiers drink and buy women for a pittance. Within a year she has a child that the US government will not take responsibility for, nor will they require the father of the child to do so.

At night she prays for God to help her and reads her Bible. She keeps it in a drawer next to her bed where she sleeps with men in order to send money home to care for her child and family. Is she a sinner? Where is God in all this systemic evil perpetrated upon an innocent girl by economic and military powers? God asks where are we? Perhaps we're planning to purchase our summer home from the wealth our nation builds on the backs of the poor across the world.

Since we are all victims of sin before we become perpetrators, the better question would be: What constitutes being a perpetrator of sin, and of evil? When are we simply living in ignorance of reality? Of course no one has ever said, "I've solved the problem of evil," ever! To face reality and learn our culpability for reality is a spiritual task most people never learn.

To recognize all women as guardians of life brings us back to the root of the problem: males have failed to produce a world consistent with God's way for humanity. Jesus loves endangered guardians and looks to his people to love them and end the abuse, to end the social structures that lead to the endangering of the guardians of life.

# God, Romance, and Legacy

### Heavenly Romance

*Ah to be loved*
*The sweet kiss of friendship and desire*
*all wrapped up in God's gift of romance*
*Loneliness sickens the soul with confusion*
*To be loved, a fairytale or a dream?*
*Overwhelming emotions ignite the flame that burns the wick of risk*
*A fool or a madman*
*Shall I always love alone?*
*Who orchestrates the heart?*
*Freedom untold,*
*to love bold or dwindle away*
*Her smile holds eternity*
*Her laugh the music of angels*
*Her tears the sorrow of all that is alone*
*What would I give?*

In the course of presenting the following ideas it might be thought that I'm a romantic whose aesthetic sense of reality lacks the intellectual rigor to think of love in psychological, biological, and cultural concepts. I must immediately deny such thoughts, for although I was captured by love long ago and reacted in unimaginable ways that affirmed love's power to preserve and bless the mutual lives of two human beings, my reflective powers on this subject is not mere romanticism. Yet, I understand romantic love to be like a force so powerful that it is overwhelming; it is like rolling thunder bellowing from heaven. It is like hearing God speak or perhaps it is God speaking.

I will begin my reflection with the scriptural statement "God is love." God gives definition to love. Of course, a person would have to grasp fully the revelation of God's love beyond the present reductionist religious thought on the meaning of the cross existent in most of America. God is *just*, but is not referenced in Scripture with *God is justice*. Justice is subject to the power of love that brings grace and mercy. Justice without love is not expressive of God; it is only penal vengeance or heavy-handed oppression on the powerless.

Love then is first a spiritual reality that flows from the creator of life. Love is a power, and it has been said that as a power *love is a weapon* when using nonviolent resistance. As a weapon love overcomes the world. How much more should you or I if we really love? I will suggest that love can exist in a human being in two distinct ways that are both dependent upon God.

First, to align with God in faith and seek God in the present is to connect with love. A person in relationship with God through faith can experience an intensified love for others, even a romantic partner, because knowing God, maturing in spirituality and wisdom, enhances the love released from God when we live out the likeness and image we bear. Second is God's love working in the world even when the faith of an individual is not present. I will explain.

I think God gives us, through likeness, and from the image of God we bear, the ability to receive love's power (and God is love). I mean that when love is functioning in relation to likeness and image then God releases the living reality of love from God's self. Love like this is not subject to religious creeds. It is God in the world without religious restriction. Faith is not at work, but love is present.

Perhaps you've felt the power and presence of love generated by being in a large group with two people whose blossoming love is easily recognizable? I have. Perhaps you have been one of those persons?

Although I've attempted to provide an understandable difference in these two manifestations of love, they are not so distinct as to always be entirely separate. One is a faith relationship that produces love; the other is associated with likeness and image-bearing.

Since God is love, then love is godlike; love is spiritual whether from faith, or living out likeness and image. Of course love from God is never immoral; rather, it is more moral than the world in which we live. Love is giving of self, even as God gives of God's self that we might love.

Love from likeness and image that is enhanced by faith's relationship with God through discerning the will of God in the forming of a romantic relationship is as real as the night sky. It has the power to create life in the world. Because we are romantic but not always theologically correct, we produce dreamy (mistaken) concepts like "soul mate." Yes, God works to aid us in our need to love and be loved by the gendered difference of the other. We need one another. When a man loves a woman he can feel it and so can she and everybody else. Xavier Zubiri might refer to this as part of our sentient intelligence. Our awareness of reality runs deeper than the things seen.

Two human beings living out their love and faith in a chaotic world is the goodness of God that inspires hope. It is the call to live in a way that displays the love of God for humanity. Their love is their legacy; it outlives them as an indomitable memory in the mind of God. The greatest love stories do not follow social mores, they are unconventional but find love in the midst of the mess.

## ROMANTIC LOVE AND SEXUALITY

It is often assumed that romantic love is to be equated with erotic love, that is, sexuality. Sexuality is foreign to God as Spirit and was not a part of the life of Jesus. Sexuality is an instinctual impulse, a drive that belongs to the physical and is not part of the likeness and image of God in which humanity is created. Romantic love enhances sexuality but is not dependent upon the sexual impulse for its origins. As I have argued, the origin of romantic love is in God.

To connect love with sexuality and not affirm the distinct separation, to fail to recognize romantic love apart from eroticism is to subject God to sexuality. As I have stated in other places, the Song of Solomon placed in the canon sanctions sexuality between a man and a woman as sacred; it is a sacredness shared between two persons. God is not involved; this is why God is not mentioned in the Song of Solomon. That marriage, sexuality, and procreation are not a part of the resurrection attests to the separation of God and humanity. When humanity's metaphorical marriage to God occurs, gender difference remains, but sexuality is lost.

## SEX AND ROMANTIC LOVE

I think it is an error to take the wonderful metaphors of Scripture that portray God as a lover of humanity and then push *the deity* aside to become an unempathic static power. God is love. It is likeness and image in relation to God that gives humanity ontological awareness and insight. Romantic love is an overwhelming power that is part of our sentience as persons. It is greater than we are when governed by goodness; the wicked mar love. If people understood that sexuality is not the driving power of romantic love, then we would witness healthier relationships in our society, even our world.

## SUMMARY

In summary, I've concluded that real love comes from God. This is so because *God is love*. Love must be moral and consistent with *likeness* and display the *image of God*. Although God is love, love is not God. God has, in my thought, released the power of his self or love into our reality. Love can be abused when not governed by faith, likeness, and image. Love received through faith's relationship is a bonus and enhances the power of love released into creation through likeness and image.

Romantic love is God's gift to male-female relationships. It is more than biology; it is God calling for two people to leave a legacy of love that communicates God's love for humanity. God is a romantic who loves us with the beauty of creation and the wonders of his desire for us. God's desire for humanity is so emotively intense that the cross is an act of love (not penal substitution which is a wretched slander against God).

So, your spouse is more important than your parents or any children born because of said relationship. Love is always from God, always God working in the world. Love that mars likeness and image, or is void of faith, has crucified God just like they did Jesus. Love's legacy is not dependent upon children, but children need a legacy of love. Only then can they overcome the world.

Love, like life, is messy. It is an adventurous gift of immeasurable wonder. Be free in Christ. Romance your spouse without shame. Happiness is lived on the edge of messy, next door to untamable, friends with the unpredictable, and mixed with tears of sorrow and joy.

To love another is to hear the dance of life as love seeks to speak. God is an ever-hopeful romantic, ever desiring for humanity to hear his voice that sings of life, love, and peace amidst the suffering of existence. Love is like the magic of touching the transcendent God and as such can only be shared in the imaginative allure of a fairy tale.

# Repairing the World at the Root

### THE LOVER'S DANCE

*In the unpredictable
the unexpected
in the step outside of normalcy
beyond the horizon of social order
calling, disrupting, challenging;
boundless love ready to surprise.
Breathe, lay aside your rules.
It's God's day and he is more.
Dance with her
to the rhythm of life.
In doing so, together you will dance with your creator,
the Lord of life.*

I AM GOING TO share a few of my related convictions. Before I state them clearly, I want to remind my reader that the only affirming evidence that a person has been recipient of a revelation is the conviction that determines their life and choices. For a person with conviction, their very being is dependent upon living true to their belief.

Conviction exists in a person when their entire being believes something to be true, to be from God, with such certainty that he or she would stand alone against the world and not relinquish their conviction. Conviction grows in revelation, it is accepted, articulated, and fills a person's life. A fully matured conviction arrests the soul and a person possessing a revelation cannot violate it. In this world, conviction is the most powerful, reality-forming proof of spirituality a person can possess. When institutions and culture fail to support the flourishing of life, a person of conviction will defy their power and choose morality in concert with their beliefs. This kind of action is common to the exemplary heroes of humanity.

It is my conviction that the healing of the world is ultimately dependent upon humanity living together as male and female; that the disjunction of relationship between the genders is at the root of all humanity's problems. It is my conviction that exhibiting the image of God through the male-female relational dynamic is the challenge set before us throughout the entirety of Scripture. The apparent misogyny of Scripture is countered by literary subversion throughout its entire corpus. Learning to read all of Scripture like Jesus is the imperative of our age.

Male dominance and the silencing of the female voice is contrary to the image of God between the genders. It mars the image of God and also silences God's voice in the world. That Abel does not speak in the Cain and Abel story is theologically instructive. The silencing of a human being's voice (in contrast to nurturing) is equivalent to murder. The failure of males to give time to the emotions of women and wait for their input in life is one of the relational problems that affect both personal and societal relationships; it is equivalent to murder through the pain and suffering of oppression.

*God's grace is as real and empowering as God's love that moves our hearts to do the impossible.*

Love's first emotion is grace. Grace is the acceptance of another person; it overlooks the flaws and weaknesses common to us all. Familiarity is the enemy of grace. It is a dangerous misperception of another person and makes human beings predictable. The inhibiting language of familiarity disables the maturation of change produced by spiritual growth. Speech patterns that address another with *You always* or *You'll never change* are inconsistent with the Christian life. Christianity resists familiarity because our faith believes in the making of a new person. Grace is always empowering whether from God or another person. Grace says, "I believe in you," it sees beyond the frailty that marks our personality and awareness of reality. It is life giving.

*Grace is love's first emotion and promises born of conviction are love's maturation.*

## SEX AND ROMANTIC LOVE

Love doesn't bloom without promises. God's unilateral, unconditional promises are accompanied with God swearing and often include a covenant ceremony that expresses the irrevocable, unalterable reality of the promise. As image-bearing creatures we are capable of making promises to one another and living out those promises through the power of conviction. Because conviction is born of revelation, our power to live out a promise is built upon our relationship, our maturity, and our dependence upon God. It is the maturity of knowing one's self that enables a person to affirm with certainty their will to keep a promise. Marriage needs ongoing promises to survive the complexities of a chaotic world.

The kind of promise-making I'm going to suggest will seem to some as beyond the realm of possibility. I do not believe this to be so. I do believe and think, however, that only a person who has had some life experience, who has grown to know their self through moments that tested their integrity, their soul, is ready to make my proposed types of promises.

These promises are built upon values, the first of which is the value (love) placed upon the recipient of the promise by the one who promises. Because God is nonviolent and anger is a monotheistic radicalism applied to God (I don't believe in an angry God), then it is good and wise to promise your loved one that you will never become angry with them.[1] Of course relationships capable of receiving this kind of a promise require mature human beings who know one another beyond mere snippets of perception.

Relationships strain to be healthy under outbursts of anger. People think that anger is a legitimate emotion. This thought is based upon poor theology and their own personal lack of self-control.[2]

> *But now you must get rid of all such things—anger, wrath, malice, slander, and abusive language from your mouth.*
> *(Col 3:8)*

If your loved one can wreck your new car and you refuse anger then your value is on the welfare of your loved one. If your value is on the car

---

1. The temptation is to make a place for justifiable anger because of some major transgression. However, when love is present and anger is no longer an option then the one promising not to succumb to anger is left only with feelings of hurt. It is important to remember I am working with the belief that two people can live out their lives with promises and not violate their relationship with a major transgression. Yet, major transgressions can also be forgiven.

2. The perceived anger of the Lord is simply his absence from a world that crucifies him daily. So, people hurt people, and nature erupts from our disharmonious existence that is contrary to the life of God.

then anger will win the day. It is the value we place on our loved ones that is able to halt anger. The preservation of a serene spirit that resists anger is a product of abiding faith in a world where the present sufferings of this age become mere temporal disruption.

For inspiring thought on promise-making to ensure the health and maturation of a male-female relationship, particularly a romantic one, I will suggest another promise. This promise is simple yet subjective because of misunderstandings; the promise is to tell your loved one that you will never hurt them. I am not even thinking about physical abuse! Rather, I am thinking of a genuine sensitivity for the feelings, emotions, and needs of the other. This promise requires that the one making the promise live for the sake of their loved one. It is irrational, it is self-sacrificial, and it is divine. We cannot love our neighbor as ourself if we cannot love our loved one with this preferential choice to live for their welfare and happiness, and not hurt them.

## LEARNING TO LISTEN

Promise to listen to your spouse, it is particularly important for the male to make this promise and the woman will listen in return. I have a little saying, "Beware Maleness." The male tendency to take, to produce immediate results, to get it done, is both good and bad. Unfortunately, when maleness is identified as only positive then it becomes insensitive and domination of others (especially women) follows. This is so in the male-female relationship because men do not take time to allow for the emotions and cautious decision-making of women. Women often hear men say, "Nevermind, I'll do it." This response ignores the female's relation to intelligence that understands change is best incorporated into life when measured carefully, with thought, and in the process emotions are given time to adjust to changing realities.[3]

---

3. It is notable that the intelligence of Adam is exhibited in naming. It is also notable that Adam does not name the woman until after the eating of the prohibited fruit. Eve's intelligence is exhibited in her aesthetic, ethical, and religious contemplation (the fruit is pleasing to the eye, it is food, and offers knowledge of the unknown). The display of Eve's introspective thought life is revealing of the intelligence of women concerning relational realities. That Adam did not name Eve until after eating the fruit is revealing of a separation between the male and the female. However, when Adam does name Eve, he relates her to godlikeness (her name in Hebrew is close in sound to the name of God). I think this is because Scripture wants us to understand that humanity's completeness is

The failure of males to listen to women based upon supposed expediency (or most other reasons) results in a break of fellowship, a disjunctive rift in a needed harmonious existence, it is to turn the dance of life into mechanics without the art of love. The annulling of the female voice is oppressive, murderous, and causes emotional harm to these gifts of God whose emotions are meant to bless and enhance our lives. The Lord, who listened to women's voices, has set the rhythm of life. There is no dance without women![4]

---

dependent upon their success to live in peace, with mutual respect as male and female, as equals. Our gendered difference is God's gift for us to experience spiritual dependency upon one another as we meet the challenges of living in a hostile environment.

4. Children learn how to relate to others, specifically the other gender, from the model exhibited in the home. A healthy home can counter the influence of errant or harmful cultural norms. This being said, culture is determined by family life.

# CATEGORY V

# POPULAR MYTHS

# Sexuality and the Metaphysical Myth of Modern Man

## Structures of Sexual Reality

*Freedom's sin*
*Humanity redefining herself*
*On the other side, away from wisdom, uncreation*
*Life's end*
*God loves erring humanity, ever calling them to wisdom, to life*
*Sexuality always sensual, never spiritual*
*a gift for pleasure*
*a gift for offspring*
*a gift to be held responsibly*
*Love doesn't come without a promise*

## Preliminary Notes for My Reader

ALTHOUGH I REJECT THE normalization of homosexuality, I am opposed to any expression of hate toward homosexual persons or the limiting of human rights in relation to homosexual persons.

In this chapter, I do not address the birth defects that contribute to confusion of sexual identity. Briefly, these incidents reflect a need for compassion and understanding that can defy accepted norms.

Some suggest celibacy within the confines of a religious order as an option for homosexual persons. Recent history has displayed, through failure, that a religious order is not sufficient to contain the desire for touch and sexual life in human beings.

The vastness of this subject in relation to individual cases is extensive, complicated, and not explored in this essay; such work belongs to case studies and statistical research efforts. We are going to need a lot of grace for this complex reality.

## THE END OF LIFE

To say that homosexuality is a created, or a natural state, is a metaphysical claim. This is so because the claim defies created biological difference and voids any impact of psychological and sociological effects on the human psyche that serve to understand homosexuality. Further, this particular claim denies the power of the will in relation to the natural biology of gender. Rather than wrestle with the responsibility of choice, or the existential ripples in humanity that contribute to gender confusion, homosexual apologists opt for a spiritual explanation that effectively normalizes their behavior with a metaphysical claim.

The misplaced *inner gender* idea relies upon the concept of *spirit*, that their spirit defines their identity and their spirit has been placed in the wrong body. So, either God is cruel and intends for some to suffer the difference of a state of existence that is in conflict with biological realities, or there are other factors to be considered.

Some justify their homosexuality under the richness of love, as though in the name of love anything can be normalized. Love does not require sexual activity. Further, the myth of the misplaced spirit makes sexuality a spiritual reality rather than belonging to the creaturely aspect of humanity. This thinking inexorably leads to the worship of sexuality and devolves religion in a return to the sex cults of the past.

It is a well-known fact that religion appeals to the human psyche and so religion is not subject to reason. However, religion wrestles with reason whereas the homosexual community's response avoids the dialectics of understanding based on a metaphysical claim and an appeal to love that disavows sexual ethics.

It is politically incorrect to speak reasonably about homosexual behavior in a society that has lost the ability to think critically about reality. Homosexuality as a created state is now a metaphysical myth; it is an unwritten, unexamined, growing myth, a myth that is without historical precedent. The current birth of this new *consciousness*, this sociological emerging of a myth without a past is indicative of a psychotic episode, even a psychotic epidemic. A psychotic episode is to redefine humanity apart from what she knows herself to be.

As an epidemic the normalization of homosexuality opens up an alternative way of living, it ignites desire as it arises from Pandora's box. Where choice and desire were once held in check by cultural and sociological taboo they are now released into the air of possibility and haunt the realm of the living like released spirits.

The resignation of same-gendered persons choosing to publicly live together as a familial unit and attempting to live ethically in society posits a situation that was once hidden; meaning homosexual couples did not flaunt their status as homosexuals but lived together quietly. The burden of secrecy and accompanying societal guilt became obstacles for these persons whose lives often demonstrated love and ethical concern for others regardless of their sexual life.

However, shame is an unpleasant if not damning aspect of sexuality and has driven many with homosexual desires to resort to suicide. We all seek acceptance, and sexuality is fraught with variations of shameful or unacceptable behavior. The guilt for failed sexual behavior is so pervasive in humanity that we all know and experience some shame; this alone should alert us to a need for grace. The current social concern for homosexual persons is inclusive of a concentrated effort to remove shame from the status of persons practicing a homosexual lifestyle.

I think we must ask if societal and religious acceptance can remove shame as an aspect of the homosexual experience. Although social and religious acceptance can ease the tension caused by outside pressures, it is unlikely that it can conquer the natural reality of shame brought on by the conflict of life at odds with natural biology.

The current normalization of homosexuality is more than a political trend; it is the recreating of humanity on a myth that has no history. The myth of homosexuality as a created state of existence is associated with the myth of progress. Not technological progress, but the myth that humanity is evolving into more than our ancestors that lived in past millennia. To embrace homosexuality as evidence of human enlightenment is at the heart of this new myth without a history.

Sociological and psychological factors affect identity formation. This being said, the normalization of homosexuality makes it an option, a choice for developing human beings. Although the metaphysical claim is that being homosexual is not a choice, the sociological effect of normalization creates a choice for persons that would otherwise not choose to live as a homosexual person.

The metaphysical claim seeks to undermine critical reflection on the historical presence of homosexuality and its current rise in American society. Critical reflection becomes an offensive task once normalization is introduced into law and the social fabric. The normalization of homosexuality posits for developing persons a choice. The lived and normalized choice becomes an object for imitation. As a result, the population of homosexual persons will increase due to the effects of normalization. This is more so due to newfound religious approval. So sexuality becomes an identity-forming power rather than a gift for male and female couples.

Under the metaphysical myth of homosexuality, the human desire for sex becomes an uncontrollable desire that breaches the natural order of gendered beings. It is for this reason that sexual restraint is taught in Christianity as a *spiritual discipline*. The menstrual cycle provides a natural time for sexual activity to halt (for both men and women), and a natural time for attending to spiritual matters in order to gain control of and over the sexual instinct.[1]

In my thinking, circumcision required in the Hebrew Scriptures is instructive for males because it is God taking ownership of the male's procreative powers and sexual behavior. Our sexual impulse, the instinctual desire for sex, must be tamed and only through spiritual discipline with an abiding love and respect for the other gender can we learn to live and have a healthy sexual life.

Human beings are mimetic; we learn through imitation. Although we are mimetic and imitate others, the biological determination that makes us gendered creatures directs our choice of which (parent) or gender we will model in relation to femaleness or maleness. Other biological factors contribute to our need and ability to imitate a specific gender's style of speech, movements, and desires. Gender identity is first biological and secondly sociocultural through perceived roles. Along with gender identity is the sexual aspect of gender behavior that is both instinctual and learned.

---

1. I think Paul had the menstrual cycle in mind when offering his advice in 1 Corinthians 7:5, but did not identify this specifically because of not wanting to exclude postmenopausal women or exclude a simple decision to practice the spiritual discipline of sexual restraint.

We are sexual beings. Like all aspects of being human, we need civil law to govern our behavior in all matters that affect all of us. Simply said, we cannot legislate morality, but we can regulate behavior. The production of a healthy society is built on human rights and personal liberty to choose. However, our choices function within boundaries defined by natural limits, e.g., a man cannot choose to bear a child.

The promotion of homosexuality as a metaphysical *myth and mystery* rather than a choice based upon desire is a reflection of a society that has failed to regulate sexual behavior in healthy ways. Also, the imposing of sexual identity through remarks challenging a person's biologically determined gender, especially at a young age, is a sociological power that imposes upon a young person a sense of a predetermined role beyond their power.

The misogyny that is pervasive in American society is rooted in ways that violate a healthy relationship with women. Misogyny is sexual dominance and disallows the equality of males and females as bearers of God's image. Further, misogyny makes the female's sexuality threatening to males. The scapegoating of females through suppression of their sensuality is done to appease the lack of sexual restraint by males and is often rejected by gentler men who are then labeled as effeminate.

Regulating all forms of sexual display is essential for a healthy society. This being said, heterosexual pornography is ultimately more detrimental to society than the presence of homosexuality.

The removal of the power of choice in the metaphysical myth annuls the spontaneity of humanity as creators of reality. Yet, the myth is a reality-building tool, an unwritten etiology; it is the fabrication of a new reality. Normalizing homosexuality alters humanity by ignoring the limits we face as gendered, reproducing, mortal beings. This is so because it defies nature.

Social structure forms human behavior and attempts to define or redefine morality. The disjunction in gender relations, our failure to live in mutually respectful ways as gendered persons, and the complexity of sexuality all contribute to an unhealthy social structure. Solving the abuse of sexuality in our society will require both regulation and redefining cultural values. As a people, we are shallow aesthetes who value appearances over character. We are a violent people whose desire for order requires severe punishment for those that are victims of a failing society built upon runaway desires.

# POPULAR MYTHS

We are now including in the structuring of society an unwritten myth of sexual orientation that is more mythically religious in nature than it is reasoned according to the biological life of gendered beings or the psychological realities of sex and shame. The metaphysical myth of homosexuality requires a god who confuses the created order with a *hybrid* person. The homosexual myth requires a god who is capricious and defies the ordering of a good creation with natural law.

The tension of a highly structured society that threatens personal liberty will produce injustice and result in collapse. The social structure of the US is a complex of fractured realities attempting to endure at the expense of our humanity. Sexuality is one of the most potently packed realities of human experience. It requires the use of wisdom and self-control. It is not a spiritual aspect of our being, but rather it requires governing from the spiritual, the religious aspect of our being. It is for this reason that theology must address the affects of all sexual expression on society.

We are sexual beings because we are gendered beings. The spiritual aspect of sexuality is not in relation to God. This is the theological error of the metaphysical myth of homosexuality. Rather the spiritual aspect of sexuality is in relation to the violation of the natural structures of creation; it is a negative relation. The spiritual aspect of homosexuality is the negation of the good, that is, to mar the creation and reduce sexuality solely to instinct rather than insight, to cast off restraint and respond only to desire. It is to be in conflict with the work of the Spirit of God the creator.

Wisdom is to cooperate with the underlying structures of reality that define humanity through the power of choice that recognizes the work of God in creation. The homosexual claim of *no choice* insists on sexual expression as an uncontrollable desire rather than as a gift.[2] Sexuality is a gift to be enjoyed. The pleasure of sex for male and female couples living to fulfill their marriage promises provides the setting for a family that creates and nurtures new life. For older couples, who (often) due to menopause in the female are no longer able to reproduce, sexuality remains a life-giving part of their relationship.

It is true that the spiritual aspect of human sexuality is in relation to the good structures of creation put in place by God, however, not in direct

---

2. If the sexual impulse is uncontrollable then the choice to abstain is impossible. That sexual restraint is a spiritual discipline affirms the need for sexuality to be governed by the religious. Sexual ethics require limits for male/female relationships where sexual behavior is naturally accommodated. The application of sexual ethics must be applied to those who identify as homosexual where sexuality is not naturally accommodated.

relation to God's Spirit, but in relation to the wisdom or voice of God discerned in the created order. God is not a sexual being. Sexuality is foreign to God's being and experience. Sexuality belongs to the creature. Jesus' celibacy indicates that engaging in sex does not contribute to the fulfilling of the image of God. Jesus will conclude that sexuality does not survive the resurrection, although gender distinctiveness will. To abuse sexual life (in any form or expression) is to participate in uncreation to oppose the wisdom of God. Sexuality belongs to the sphere of the sacred between a male and a female.

## Love Doesn't Come Without a Promise

The spirituality of marriage is in the promise, the relationship, not the sexual act. God is not involved, does not participate, and does not violate the sphere of the sacred between a male and a female. Human sexuality is love and worship of the other, not love and worship of God. This is portrayed in the Song of Solomon, a book that celebrates male and female sexuality. The absence of God in the Song of Solomon is confirming of human sexuality as sacred apart from God. The inclusion of the Song of Solomon in the canon affirms that sexuality is sacred within the context of marriage as male and female.

The error of Israel's neighbors was to attribute sexuality to their god(s), to worship their god(s) through the spiritualizing of sexuality. The metaphysical claim that homosexuality is a natural state from birth due to a gendered spirit in the wrong body is to spiritualize sexuality. It is a subtle return to the ideologies of the sex cults of the past.

Sex is not sin. However, uncontrolled sexual desire that eradicates the natural limits of gender is sin. Unrestrained sexuality that functions without a promise, or without concern for progeny is a sin. This does not annul the joy of sexual life for those persons who have passed beyond child-bearing years or who experience infertility and live out the promise of marriage. The potency of sexuality for life is matched by its potency for self-destruction. We are living in a moment when the need to understand sexual restraint as wisdom, as a spiritual discipline of profound importance, is imperative. Sexual restraint for purposes of seeking spirit*ual matters* is revealing of the image of God in the Lord's people; this too can be abused if it is removed from a couple's personal choice to be governed by any authority, whether civil or religious.

In conclusion, I do not think that homosexual relationships should be normalized through the institution of marriage. The concept of marriage as an institution belongs to religion and not the state. Homosexual relationships should be acknowledged in civil law to protect their rights as persons, but the word *marriage* belongs to religious faith and to male and female relationships.

## Love and Truth Walk Together

I live in the Philippines and interact with homosexual persons nearly everyday, at the gym, waiting in the dentist office, at restaurants, coffee shops, medical clinics, hospitals, while shopping, and when watching entertainers. My immediate response is empathy. They, like many heterosexual persons, are wrestling with the problem of sexuality.

Empathy and our God require we live with grace in relation to those persons whose desire for the same gender dominates their sexual impulse. Our faith requires we wrestle with a reality that challenges us at the core of our identity as human beings and side with biological identity as the way of wisdom.

Touch and affection are a part of being human and belong to all of us. A sexual relationship is subject to the ethical and the religious. Religion fails when it accepts same-gendered sex as normative, ethical, and religiously sanctioned. This is also true for acceptance of all forms of pernicious sexual behavior. We all must control our sexual desires; this includes those persons whose desire is for the same sex.

## Chapter Addendum

The lack of sexual ethics in all aspects of human behavior is a subject that is an immediate need in Christian theology. Homosexual persons have been disqualified from the pursuit of God based on their sexual desire while other unethical sexual behavior by various groups is ignored.

Throughout history the conquering of a people has always included sexual access to the women by the conquering soldiers. The US has caused untold and unexplored harm to various nations and peoples through the invading presence of the US military. US military presence in Vietnam, Thailand, and the Philippines has birthed both an international sex industry and harmed the sexual ethics of large segments of these societies.

In these locations, where sexual ethics are nonexistent, US soldiers leave behind children and acquire a sense of male power over the sexuality of women that is contrary to a healthy male role in relation to women. The language of male misogyny is acquired and nurtured in the US military. US veterans bring home the effects of living without sexual ethics. Of course, it is unnatural for men to be living in mass and without women. The military is a breeding ground for sexual colloquialisms and all types of unethical sexual behavior.

The proliferation of pornography and its deleterious affects on society is altogether ignored by those who scapegoat peaceful homosexual persons. Empathy can be given to those who suffer a misdirected desire but those who profit from abusive sexuality should be punished by legal regulations. If those who scapegoat homosexual persons for producing social ills do not address the economic injustice of the sex industry they only exhibit ignorance and their own shame.

# The Myth of Race

### We Will Be One

*We are one through an inner image*
*Our inner image, sacred*
*Our outer image, all-beautiful*
*Every face an incomparable work of art*
*Every smile cries out family*
*Every heart needs love*
*We are of one Spirit*
*God our creator*
*Anything else is shadows*

ON ONE OF MY trips to the Philippines I was swimming with a group of very agile and adept swimmers. They were all young boys who spent the day at the beach to cool off. I also was there to cool off. Whenever I'm at the beach, if a group of young children are around, they eventually want me to toss them in the air. Of course I'm always happy to enjoy their exuberant energy and laughter.

On one occasion I tossed a little fellow about ten years old into the air multiple times. He enjoyed staying under water and swimming around before coming up. I would duck under the water to see if he was okay and he would be swimming like a fish. When he came up I said to him, "Kayong lumangoy tulad ng isang isda," meaning "You swim like a fish." He responded in English, "I'm not fish, I'm people." I laughed and responded, "Yes you are people!"

In my life, experiences like this one link me to a moment, echo in my ears, and I know it is God who has spoken to me through another. As a person with a family of beautifully mixed persons, my sensitivity to the hovering spirit of racism that engulfs humanity has become a finely tuned instrument of resistance. We are all the same. We are people.

*Racism is a parasite on the soul that infects it with intolerable violence.*

A Christian cannot be a follower of Jesus and a racist. Sadly, many persons, particularly in the US, are not aware of the framing of culturally diverse peoples into a system of thought that promotes whiteness, meaning the view on people begins with whiteness as the point of departure, anything else is devolution from the norm. I will provide an example. On numerous occasions when discussing the myth of race a well-meaning person will ask, "How did the black race come about?"[1] The question assumes that light-skinned persons were the first human beings.[2] It indicates a separation from other persons that implies superiority.

> *The man named his wife Eve, because she was the mother of all living.*
> *(Gen 3:20)*

The view of theology on the human family is that we are all related; we are one species. Further, any misuse of Scripture to denigrate a group of people must also exalt the other as more *godlike*. However, theology teaches us that all humanity was created in the image and likeness of God.

> *When the LORD your God thrusts them out before you, do not say to yourself,*
> *"It is because of my righteousness that the LORD has brought me in to occupy this land"; it is rather because of the wickedness of these nations that the LORD is dispossessing them before you.*
> *(Deut 9:4)*

---

1. I do not want to entertain the ignorant readings of Scripture that have fueled hate and racism, so I will limit to a footnote this egregious abuse of Scripture. The original and abhorrent Dayke's Bible records the myths of an era that is passing away: Cain's mark, the curse of Ham (actually Canaan). Cain's mark was an act of God's love and mercy to prevent another Cain from rising by claiming he had killed Cain. This is clearly seen in Lamech, the first polygamist who turns the mercy of God into protection for murderers. Canaan in the Noah story represents Israel's prejudice toward the Canaanites as promiscuous people and ignores Israel's complicity in the same behavior as the cause for their expulsion from the land.

2. History and anthropology both affirm that humanity's earliest civilizations were all persons whose skin was not white. The theory of evolution remains a theory and inapplicable to the movements of people that spread across the earth from Mesopotamia.

In light of Israel's history, this piece from Deuteronomy is instructive for relationships with other people groups. Deuteronomy 9:4 teaches that the tendency of a people to view reality through a lens of superiority over others based upon successful domination of land results in severing relationship with God. It is a sin, a perennial threat to peace, and a perennial power that infects humanity. It is the sin of America in the failed Christianity of manifest destiny.

Israel's exile affirms they were not different from their neighbors even though they had received the revelation of God through their history; they failed to be the people of God and became only a nation-state. In the end, they lost their land but became a people who were landless for the next two millennia and in the process they learned that there is only one God.

## IMPROPER WORDS THAT HARM

Some words have a history and a specific use that are rooted in hate and are inconsistent with truth and goodness; "miscegenation" is such a word. Mixed-race or miscegenation laws flourished in the US from the seventeenth century until 1967, when the Supreme Court ruled them to be unconstitutional. Although a number of states had repealed anti-miscegenation laws there were sixteen states whose laws stood until they were over turned by the 1967 Supreme Court decision. The list of persons it was illegal for a white person to marry in these last sixteen states included Blacks, Asians, Filipinos, American Indians, Native Hawaiians, and the encompassing phrase "all nonwhites." Some persons argue that our differences in appearance were set up by God as natural boundaries to prohibit race mixing, but this is not so.

The scriptural perspective on the division of humanity into groups of people is built on two realities. First is the natural development of language that occurs when we live in groups. Language spoken in the daily lives of people will morph and produce other languages. It is an act of violence to restrain or control the human capacity to create language. It is the sin of empire.

Second, diversity of language divides people. The Babel story, through the confusion of multiple languages, prohibits the centralization of power that would result in brick-building slavery for some and towers for others. God's resistance to empire is the creative act of language in the human family. Learning another language is a humane act that has possibilities for greater understanding and peace.

Paul makes his case before the Greeks in Athens and asserts that the natural boundaries of the earth provide for dwelling places where human beings can search for God. The natural boundaries of language and geographic separation are God's effort to provide freedom from empire:

> *From one ancestor he made all nations to inhabit the whole earth,*
> *and he allotted the times of their existence and the boundaries of*
> *the places where they would live, so that they would search for God*
> *and perhaps grope for him and find him—though indeed he is not*
> *far from each one of us. For "In him we live and move and have our*
> *being"; as even some of your own poets have said,*
> *"For we too are his offspring."*
> *(Acts 17:26-28)*

The endogamy of the patriarchs is an antisocial practice and inhibits the basic intention of marriage, which is to incorporate difference into family experience. Difference brings growth both culturally and intellectually. Mixed marriages in Israel's history are a constant.

Joseph married an Egyptian woman and Moses married a Midianite. Both men are examples of marrying across linguistic and geographic boundaries. They were both multilingual and multicultural. Historically, Joseph is Israel's first wise man and Moses their first prophet. Abraham is referenced as a prophet, but his status as a prophet is revealed through the life of faith that is his story. The latter prohibitions of Nehemiah and Ezra were cruel acts of nationalist power forced upon the people in a setting that itself was a failure.

Jeremiah 16 affirms that God's intent for the outcome of Israel's exile and diaspora was to produce a people who knew that there is but one God. The exile and diaspora resulted in the loss of Hebrew as a living language; it was known only by academics (scribes, rabbis, Pharisees, and Sadducees). The result was the translation of the Hebrew language into Greek, the language of empire.

In exile, the Hebrews learned that language is not sacred. Hebrew communities existed in parts of the ancient Near East and did not return to the land; they learned that neither they nor their God were limited to a land. It was the exiles on a celebratory visit during Pentecost who heard the preaching of the apostles and became the first missionaries. In this sense the exiles of the diaspora fulfilled the will of God rather than those who returned to the land.

Although promises of land are present in the hope pieces of the poetry of the biblical prophets, the land as promise evolves into an ideal spiritual reality. Zion in the prophets will reach a height beyond any mountain in the world.[3] The mountain of God will be in Israel and the spiritual reality of God's revelation will fill the earth:

> *In days to come*
> *the mountain of the LORD's house*
> *shall be established as the highest of the mountains,*
> *and shall be raised above the hills;*
> *all the nations shall stream to it.*
> Isa 2:2

As a literary motif, the land is established by the presence of people who live in a relationship of peace and life with God and one another, a life marked by the teaching of the Torah. For the Christian the motif of exile becomes a metaphor for our spiritual lives because the present state of the world is to be transformed into a paradise where the voice of God walks with us and Jesus' reign is lived out in each person. Jesus doesn't need a throne to be Lord, nor a mountain.

It is theologically correct to say that God desires a people who seek to transform the world without the constructs of a nation-state, but rather as multicultural and multilingual people who teach ethical monotheism. The story of Israel as God's hope is fulfilled through the life-giving Spirit of Christ Jesus who is an exemplar to be followed. It is theologically correct to say Jesus embodied the call of Israel and in effect became the manifest hope of God for humanity, that is, it is God's hope and God's work that seek to conform every human being to the way of Jesus. It is theologically correct to say that God desires a people who marry across the natural boundaries of language, mountains, and seas to incorporate the nations into the family of God.

## LITTLE EMPIRES

Every nation-state is a little empire where the centralization of power limits the lives and freedoms of its inhabitants. The movement of a nation-state away from war and toward the flourishing of its entire people is a positive

---

3. Mt. Zion is only 2,510 feet. Literalist readings miss the spiritual reality of God's desire for a people that is inclusive of every human being to spring from the revelation of God, flowing from Abraham to Moses to Paul, a revelation completed in Jesus Christ the Lord.

sign. The abolishing of extreme wealth disparity, accomplished through the forgiveness of debt, demonstrates that a society respects one another. The act of resisting war, eradicating crippling debt, and caring for the least of these is consistent with the reign of Christ. This is so even if such a nation does not profess Jesus. In this sense humanism comes closer to Christian faith than some alleged practitioners of Christianity. However, humanist practices alone do not constitute the reign of God. The reign of God requires the teaching of the one God and the good news of God's joining creation as one of us.

The bride of Christ lives in exile. She is multilingual and she is a mixture of people across the earth. Paul's sole restriction on marriage is that a follower of Jesus marries another follower of Jesus. Such advice, accompanied with the boundary-crossing ministry of Jesus' followers to all humanity, is a stamp of goodness on so-called multiracial marriage. To learn the language of another people in order to share Christ with them is an act of love. To marry one of their people is to identify with them as Christ has identified with us in his becoming flesh.

As exiles our allegiance is always to God and not the state. Our marriages reflect the oneness of humanity. Like Abraham, we live, die, and bury our dead in a land of promise, a promise that is now but not yet. For the Christian there is but one race, the human race, and any other construction of humanity is evil.

The exclusionary practice of identifying a person by their appearance and labeling him/her into a racial group is contrary to the will of God. It is language and cultural moorings that aid in our likeness for personal relationships, not appearance. A multicultural person in a healthy marriage that bridges language and culture produces people who are open to understanding difference. These people help us see what we miss in the beauty of difference; difference that God created for securing places of peace free from those persons who seek to govern the entire earth.

To classify the children of cross-cultural marriages along ideas of race, which is solely based upon appearance, is unconscionable. These persons are treasures of a love that recognizes we are one humanity, we are people. They wear the beauty of difference united in their souls. I love them all. They are my children.

# The Myth of Progress

### Still the Same

*Same ole problems*
*Nothing has changed*
*Still afraid*
*Still need to be loved*
*Always a war somewhere*
*Always on the threshold of war*
*We have not learned to love*
*We have not become morally better than those who came before.*

THE ONSET OF RAPID technological advance (along with Darwinian thought) has led to the idea that humanity is progressing. This *myth of progress* supposes that because we have conquered aspects of science and physics we can rise above the violence of our own history. All hope for humanity under the myth of progress is focused on the human capacity to dominate our environment. The underlying drives of this type of progress are the survival instinct, fear of death, desire for comfort, and resource consumption. The missing component in this endeavor is essential for progress and that is faith in God.

*The object of faith in the myth of progress is the human capacity to survive, coupled with Darwinian influence.*

Survival is driven by fear, but human development is achieved by conformation to the image of God in Christ Jesus. Fear of God is liberating because it resists a person's at-all-costs desire for survival, inhibits fear of death, and subjects comfort and consumption to a responsible ethic of love toward all people. Fear of God lived out also releases a person from fear as debilitating and results in a healthy fear that often melts away in the embrace of God as father. When God in Christ Jesus is the object of faith, self-giving love is the result. Self-giving is not mere empathic response or thoughtless sacrifice. Rather, self-giving is spiritually empowered action exhibiting the wisdom of God. Occasionally the wisdom of God is perceived as foolishness because God's wisdom functions through weakness mixed with power, but not force or violent coercion.

The myth of progress is without theological insight from the revelation of God in nature, Scripture, or in Christ Jesus. For this reason the myth suffers visions of grandeur that require sacrificing large groups of humanity to its ever-consuming need for more.[1] The goal of the myth of progress is not to make humanity better, it is to make humanity technologically dominant, even dominated by technology, rather than learning to escape the boundaries of human life by knowing the power of resurrection in one's soul. Yet, to be human is to die. Jesus' humanity is affirmed by his death. Jesus' deity is affirmed through God raising him from the dead.

In the last book of Scripture, death is the enemy of God. However, death began as God's judgment on humanity's existence. The first humans could not accept life as a gift, as dependent upon the invisible God whose voice walked with them in the garden of life, the garden of God. They longed to possess life of their own volition and power. However, because death has become God's enemy, God has overcome death in Jesus Christ's authentic human life. Acceptance of death as normative and living a life in the fear of God are only possible because of the resurrection. The myth of progress is not subject to the will of God.

It is the voice of God in the human soul that objects to death. Yet, humanity is defined by birth, aging, and death. The avoidance of death as normative to the human experience results in all sorts of unethical activity that supports the myth of progress. God created humanity in order that they might become children of God, not simply by creative fiat but through a life subject to pain, suffering, and death.

---

1. The sacrificing of the powerless is justified in the mind of the powerful through belief in a self-possessed and evolved superiority. The belief is often subtle; once it rises to outward expression, the idol of nationalism becomes a vehicle for identifying membership.

POPULAR MYTHS

## HUMANITY HAS NOT PROGRESSED

Technological progress has only made us more dangerous to one another. It has only heightened our separation from one another. The normalization and multiplication of nuclear weaponry threatens all humanity. People on the other side of the world, who sit in an air-conditioned room then go home at night to their family in the suburbs, can operate drones that deploy hellfire missiles. Human barbarity has been sanitized by technology. All the horror of war is removed by distance, and reality is muddled by lifelike war games. Personal culpability for one's actions is hidden in the patriotic cleanliness of it all.

> *We are losing our humanity to sanitized violence, and programming our children to value the useless distractions of technology and the vanity of fame.*

We have not become more intelligent; we just know more stuff and none of that knowledge has made us better human beings. We have not evolved. We have not changed. The search for meaning has been replaced with the pursuit of happiness. To become spirit has been replaced with the desire for instant gratification.

## BECOMING HUMAN/BECOMING SPIRIT

Becoming human and becoming spirit are intertwined activities. Spiritual activity is not ephemeral personal experience; it is accomplished in tangible acts of love. Personal spiritual experience is validated by observable choices, pursuits, and responses in everyday life. Private times of prayer and contemplation are preparation for becoming spirit. To become spirit is to live in a manner that displays John's use of the phrase "eternal life."

In John's gospel eternal life is not merely a result or an end yet to come, rather eternal life is faith's resilience against evil and the fear of death. A person who has become spirit is not bound by the violence of the world but is released from, and releases, the presence of the reign of God into the now.

> *Becoming human and becoming spirit bring God into the world.*

To become human is to honor the image of God in us, an image we are all capable of displaying. The image of God in us is those finer attributes of being human lived out in relation to all reality. Faith, redemption, reconciliation, self-control, creative acts of imagination concretized into the world through words, keeping promises, and love—these are all aspects of the image of God and belong to the realm of both flesh and spirit.

# CATEGORY VI

# BEING POOR/BEING HUMAN

# The Sign of the Poor

*To ignore the poor is to show contempt for both God and Humanity.*

### The Poor: A Sign We Are Not Yet Saved

*Jesus belongs to the poor*
*Jesus came to liberate the poor,*
*from oppressive idols of power*
*To fail to love the poor*
*Is to worship idols*
*To end poverty*
*is to heal the world*
*Only the poor understand Jesus' suffering*

THE SIGN OF THE poor in a world of wealth demands that all who know God seek to liberate the poor. The work to liberate the poor from systemic structures of power is consistent with the heart of the God who hears the cries of the afflicted. All theology is the study of God in relation to humanity. This is so because God is a relational, redeeming creator who binds his very self to humanity with words that form promises. God's holiness is affirmed by his promise-keeping. To speak of God apart from spoken or unspoken relational realities is to halt at the categories of mystery and transcendence. Neither of these is practical for healing the world since they both exist outside the sphere of human existence.

> *It is the sign of the poor that means national leaders who rule systems of power and government have failed to serve those they are meant to represent.*

Jesus brought the reality of the reign of God into the world through his person and *koinonia* with the Holy Spirit. God entered the world as a human being and that human being brought God into the world by living a life and teaching a way that fulfilled the image of God in a human life. Death is the terminal illness that besets all of humanity's efforts at self-governance. Only in Christ Jesus can a human being overcome the eclipse of death that permeates our reality. To face death as *spirit* is to love humanity with an indomitable hope rooted in the faith of God, who raises the dead. To face death is to expose the systemic structures of human governance to the demands of love—love for God and love for neighbor.

To love God and neighbor is to be aided by contemplation of the Scriptures for the purpose of bringing God into the world. This is so because Scripture contains the revelation of God. When God is present, then the justice that liberates the poor and oppressed is present. When truth is present, concepts of righteousness based upon power and conformation to legal structures that sustain poverty and oppression are exposed as evil. Justice in the Scripture is not penal; it is merciful and healing. Justice is a relational word that brings equity into economic affairs so that no one is born into a debtor nation to suffer, so that no one suffers an oppressive social structure that inhibits their development as a human being.

*The presence of the poor across the earth testifies to the injustice existent in economic systems.*

The contemplation prevalent in the Scriptures concerns the human predicament in relation to God and the temporal powers of humanity's institutions of governance. So, the person who studies and knows Scripture is prepared to apply a living and present theology to the injustice in the world. The "sign of the poor" is the injustice that calls for theological application so that the world might be healed. To contemplate the predicament of the poor, to wrestle with the powers that oppress, is the demand of theological practice. The healing of the world begins with the liberation of the poor, and not through those who hold power but by the will of the populace. Liberation of the poor restructures cultural practices, legal systems, and moves government toward a more humane order. To practice liberation of the poor as a public responsibility is to align humanity with the will of God.

*The failure to abolish poverty is a statement on the morality of existing power structures.*

## The Sign of the Poor

To give voice to the poor is the task of theology that matters to both God and in the everyday affairs of life for most of humanity. In order to give voice to the poor it is required that the liberative worker listen to the poor, record their stories, and work for them as an intermediary voice challenging the powerful. When a liberative worker lifts up the poor through educational awareness on the structures that oppress, then the poor begin to gain their own voice. Education is at the heart of liberative efforts to empower the voice of the poor.

The church that does not stand beside or position itself alongside the poor will gravitate toward an errant theology that justifies oppression, supports unjust gain, and will bring shame upon the Christian faith. When the challenge of faith's call to heal the world with Jesus' kingdom is replaced with therapeutic sermons then a static religion of self-help makes people easy prey for idolatry and empty theology. Theology that cannot be embodied and/or bring challenge to change the world is simply useless. Remember, loving God is inseparable from loving the poor.

## THE EARTH IS THE LORD'S

*The earth is the LORD's, and the fullness thereof;*
*the world, and they that dwell therein.*
*(Ps 24:1)*

God created the world for human beings to live upon and so they could become children of God. We are caretakers of God's earth, God's land. We share the earth with one another. Sharing is relational; it works functionally as a sign of love for others. Not only is the world claimed as the Lord's in Psalm 24, but all of life and, in particular, human beings. Life is a gift and our temporality is to be received as an essential experience preparing us for the gift of life in the resurrection.

Leviticus 23:22 requires a landowner to leave the corners of his field for the poor to harvest. The legislation is rich with meaning. First, I will work from the translations that prefer *corner* rather than *edges* to designate the area to be left untouched by harvesters. Nature is without natural squares.[1]

---

1. The significance of the squared city in Revelation is indicative of God's acceptance of humanity's need for defined limits. That the city is clear as glass and the symbolism of the city is rich in metaphor indicates the success of humanity to live together as one in Christ.

The Lord has Abraham build altars in the land that are not squared. They are built of stones that have not been chiseled. Abraham lives in the land of promise as a foreigner and the only piece of land recognized by others as his is a graveyard he purchased.

Abraham's life is instructive; the only land we truly own is the piece we become a part of as our body decomposes. Memorial sites with extravagant displays do not mark Abraham's life; rather, Abraham's life is preserved as story both verbally and in writing. When land is farmed it is squared for irrigation rows. So, it is consistent with farming practices to recognize a square by corners rather than edges.

The Levitical legislation does not specify the size of the corner to be marked off. If a corner were marked off it would be done so with a line. Where to place the line is left to the decision of the landowner. At this point human culpability for interpreting the intention of the Levitical legislation comes into play. How much of the corner will be left? I think the intention is that the owner is to provide enough of the land for the poor who are dependent upon (due to proximity) the corners for their food. If this requires the landowner to mark off a large area and be left with a smaller portion in order to meet the needs of the poor then this is to fulfill the intent of the legislation. Leviticus 23:22 is about sharing and maintains the spirit of Psalm 24:1. *The land (ha-aretz) is the LORD's.*

Human beings continually square the world with lines that reach upward to the sky and outward to mark our possession of land. It is interesting to note that across the world the remnants of civilizations mark the countryside. Often these civilizations remain a mystery because their stories have not been preserved, their ideas and history not written.

The first city was built on the foundation of murder, of fratricide. The first city was built by a man (Cain) who, in spite of being a murderer, was marked by God with a sign of hope for reconciliation. The first empire is referenced in the Babel story and it was left to crumble under the design of God. The Babel story reveals to us that language in all of its continually changing, untamable use resists the centralization of power. Diversity is God's design for humanity. Embracing differences and language-learning is healthy for us. All of history and reality is about God's creating a people to be his children, a people of diversity, embracing difference and sharing the earth.

The invisible (clear as glass) city of Revelation is squared, denoting its humanness. The metaphors abound in the description of the city, gates of pearl and streets of gold. The pearl begins as an irritating speck of dirt, much like the children of God. The trying of our faith is more precious than gold so the path we walk in the city of God is depicted as streets of gold. The embrace of humanity with our limits, with our need to measure and control, is healed and embraced into the spiritual city of God. Humanity, flesh, is to be embraced into the Lord Jesus Christ to be qualified as spirit. The city of God is people living out the governance of God in a world without poverty, a world where chaos has been abolished and death forgotten.

## LITERACY AND THE POOR

The enemy of poverty is education.[2] Once a person is educated they possess something that cannot be taken away. An educated populace rejects social stratification built upon concepts of superiority. The powers of social stratification have always used economics to keep people in ignorance. Education is a human right because education is a societal responsibility to be fulfilled in the life of every human being. Education is not *job training* or assimilation into the existent powers of governance. Education is the power to think critically about reality and access the literature of humanity that records history and the laws that govern us along with philosophy, science, and other aspects of empowering knowledge.

A literate person, an educated person, filled with the hope of God, is an indomitable force and it doesn't matter how much money they do or do not have. In the economy of God, education is an imperative to be provided to every person. Without a public school system, Jesus learned to read. It is the distraction of entertainment that increases the void of ignorance. Entertainment is for the affluent, celebrity is a cruel device that leaves undeveloped people, but reading produces prophets.

A literate, educated person possesses a sense of self that cannot be silenced or humiliated. This empowering sense of self is an equalizer that resists all forms of social stratification designed to exclude a person or a group of people from the flourishing of the earth. A literate, educated person is empowered with courage and cannot be held in the grips of fear by legalized injustice.

---

2. A proper education is holistic and embraces the humanities along with schooling for a particular profession.

# BEING POOR/BEING HUMAN
## THE VIOLENCE OF POVERTY

The sign of the poor is the interpretive lens for understanding the theology needed to heal the world. Theological need is subject to human need. Theology's purpose is to serve the poor because, as I have said, the liberation of the poor is essential for the healing of the world in order to create a world without social stratification, a world where sharing the earth and all its life-giving resources is a guiding ethic and love for the poor is the call of God.

Poverty is an avoidable act of violence when it is the result of systems and institutions of power. Poverty can only be maintained by injustice. The presence of systemic poverty is war on humanity by humanity; it is madness, greed, complacency, godless, and intolerable for people of faith. The violence of nature we cannot entirely control, but we can control our response. Poverty by any cause is an intolerable condition which is to be healed by everyone through sharing our resources with the afflicted.

The chasm faced by the rich man was of his own construction. It was a chasm of indifference, of calloused comfort, unable to contend with the call of God in human reality to lift up the poor. His picture in hades is of a condition. His condition was self-consuming; he awoke in the afterlife as an incomplete human being. He still would not, or could not, weep for Lazarus. James warns of a form of misery that will come upon the rich. He does not explain what those miseries will be. Will it be the eternal call of God to love the poor man at rest in Abraham's bosom?

# Forever Human

### When Power Finds its Place

*When power finds its place*
*the defining event*
*light to guide the world*
*healing unimagined*
*Chaos captured*
*Dragons no more*
*Peace, justice, life, reign*
*Jacob so small*
*Galilee a hamlet of nobodies*
*God has become Man*
*When power finds its place*
*Likeness and image abound*
*Listen, a rumbling deep in the throes of existence*
*The voice of God*
*Up from the earth*
*A quaking*
*It's only a child*
*When power finds its place*
*Life born of death*
*Hear, for the earth, quakes like Sinai*
*A man rises*

GOD NEVER LOSES US. In the absence of the body, all that constitutes our existence is held in the loving Spirit of God. God's act of joining the creation by making part of what it means to be God to be human affirms God's desire for us to live. Jesus does not intend to be alone!

> *The LORD has sworn and will not change his mind,*
> *"You are a priest forever according to the order of Melchizedek."*
> *(Ps 110:4)*

Psalm 110 was written to preserve two oracles. The first is in verse one, and the second is in verse four. The psalm is eschatological, attending to the final victory of God through the *Adonai* (Lord) who reigns. Verse 1 begins with an older speech formula *neum* (says) and gives the oracle a sense of antiquity.[1] This particular verse is the most oft-quoted OT verse in the NT.[2] This being said, the importance of understanding verse 1 in its setting and in its NT use is imperative for NT theology.

Jesus' use of the verse is to deny that the Lord is a son of David. This alone has important repercussions on interpreting the purpose, use, and legitimacy of the Davidic covenant.

> *Now while the Pharisees were gathered together, Jesus asked them this question: "What do you think of the Messiah? Whose son is he?"*
> *They said to him, "The son of David."*
> *He said to them, "How is it then that David by the Spirit calls him Lord, saying,*
> *'The Lord said to my Lord,*
> *"Sit at my right hand, until I put your enemies under your feet?"'*
> *If David thus calls him Lord, how can he be his son?" No one was able to give him an answer, nor from that day did anyone dare to ask him any more questions.*
> *(Matt 22:41–46)*

Jesus used this piece of Scripture to challenge the religious leaders of his day over the identity of the expected Messiah. They wanted someone like David. Jesus clarifies that the Messiah is unlike David; the Messiah is greater than David. Jesus identifies the role of the Lord in Psalm 110 in a subversive form: Jesus is the Lord of Psalm 110.

---

1. The common speech formula is *ci amar* YHWH, whereas Psalm 110:1 uses an older speech formula *neum* YHWH. This usage is indicative of the age of the oracles.

2. Psalm 110:1 is used in the following places in the NT: Matt 22:44; 26:64; Mark 12:36; 14:62; 16:19; Luke 20:42; 22:69; Acts 2:34; Rom 8:34; 1 Cor 15:25; Eph 1:20; Col 3:1; Heb 1:3, 13; 8:1; 10:12. Psalm 110:4 is used in: Rom 11:29; Heb 5:6, 10; 6:20; 7:3, 11, 15, 17, 21.

The Lord (*Adonai*) in the psalm is portrayed as equal to the LORD (*YHWH*) invited to sit at his right hand. He is addressed by the LORD as the manifestation of the LORD on the earth and among human beings.

In the second oracle of verse 4, the LORD swears. In the Davidic covenant, Nathan's God speech does not contain the word "swear." When God swears, he is making the words he speaks irrevocable:

> *The LORD has sworn and will not change his mind,*
> *"You are a priest forever according to the order of Melchizedek."*
> Ps 110:4

In Scripture, when God changes his mind, he does not *shub*, which means "repent." Rather, the word used is *naham*, a word rooted in the idea that if God does change his mind on a matter it is because of compassion for us. However, in verse 4, the LORD swears he will not change his mind. I think this is because his compassion for humanity is to provide us with what we need. We need a Lord who is one of us, who understands us through experiencing being human. This Lord's role as our priest is forever. So, the incarnation of God is not an experiment; it is not a temporary role, it is God joining the adventure of life as one of us. It is permanent. There has been change in God. He has added being human to God's sense of self. God's character does not change; his nature remains holy, but being human is added to who God is. He is the Christ.

That the existence of being human is possible for God is because humanity is created in his likeness and image. So, although there is a *kenosis* (self-emptying), through this act the transcendent invisible God (*YHWH*) can be seen. God has become one of us. Being human has been incorporated into the being of God. For this reason, we too can, through our Lord, our Priest, be embraced into the being of God because the Christ fills all that God is. Humanity has touched God.

This understanding of Psalm 110 brings wonderful assurance to us all. Our existence is before our essence; we are alive. God will never lose us. Jesus will have a family. God keeps each one of us.

The preservation of our bodies is irrelevant in relation to the preservation of our living existence. Absent from the body we are present with the Lord. God keeps us and death cannot end our existence. Whether the writer had intentions for thoughts of resurrection and incarnation to be a part of the psalm seems to me irrelevant because the writer is preserving two oracular statements.

The independence of these statements from the rest of the psalm is witnessed by their use in the NT. That the first oracle is so important to the NT through quotes and obvious allusions confirms the oracle's distinctiveness. The verses that surround these two oracular statements affirm and compliment the oracle's words. Without the statements, the other verses are void of interpretive context. The oracular statements can stand alone in the NT. Finally, it is Jesus who provides interpretive meaning to the entire psalm.

Our culture is adrift without introspection; this spirit of apathetic conformity permeates the religious practices of our people. We are (overall) a people who prefer order at the cost of justice. Our religious thought has become (overall) both supportive of inhumane behavior and faithless—dependence upon God, upon the way of Jesus, is replaced with trust in powers that are in direct opposition to the will of God. This is so because militarism, materialism, and nationalism combine to create the state religion and the combination is particularly at home in evangelicalism.

The martyrs knew that you can burn my body but this act will not stop my resurrection. They believed Jesus rose physically, that after the throes of death Jesus had won and in victory ascended into the realm of God. Metaphorically seated at the right hand of God, the Lord reigns. The martyrs understood life's temporal journey is preparation for new life with a loving, nonviolent God. They knew that how we live is more important than what we think we know. They knew that following Jesus involves every part of life and cannot be compartmentalized.

If we spent less time on quick-fix conversion and more time learning to be followers of Jesus, our witness would change the world. The communication of the gospel has been reduced to formulaic confession that is void of the depth of God's revelation in the Lord Jesus Christ. This being said, Christianity is not taught because it is lost in a simplistic formula. Simplicity is not a problem unless it becomes formulaic for religious claims of inclusion or exclusion.

God has become forever human and forever human we will remain. To learn to be a human being is at the heart of all religion, and Jesus (the son of man) is the most excellent example of being human who has ever lived. We are loved of God and he will hold us and never lose us. He will resurrect us to dance upon a new earth of heavenly origin, for God loves his creation.

# CATEGORY VII

# FORGIVENESS

# Forgiving God

## The World Doesn't Work Without Forgiveness

*The world doesn't work without forgiveness*
*Forgiveness is divine*
*Birthed in God's desire*
*To not be alone*
*One God*
*Many children*
*If God needed nothing*
*After creation*
*God needed humanity*
*This is the cost unimaginable*
*Eternity endures because of forgiveness*

FORGETTING IS A UNIVERSAL human experience. Without the help of friends, photographs, and videos to help us recall events, as the decades pass, a few years of life can be reduced to thirty minutes of storytelling. We forget more than we remember. In Scripture, the word "remember" sits in contrast to the word "forget." The Scripture commands us to not forget God's covenants, God's acts, and the poor.

The significance of the word "remember" in the Old Testament is marked by its location and connection to the word "covenant." In effect we are to remember God's promises, both conditional and unconditional. There are also many calls to remember the acts of God, particularly in the Exodus event.

The Scripture, by example, is instructive on the importance of training the memory for the sake of self-understanding. Self-understanding is accomplished through remembering

Self-reflection, along with the forming and telling of personal stories, is a universal human activity. It is how we communicate who we understand ourselves to be. It is a healthy activity to collect one's own personal experiences into a melody of storytelling that helps others on their life journey.

Some memories, particularly memories of abuse or traumatic experiences, can capture the power of memory and bind us to a moment for the rest of our lives. Learning to hold these memories as part of our history but not as definitive of our value or role as a human being requires the accumulation of redeeming stories from the life of the victim, the life of others, and Scripture. Scripture is a valuable aide, with its many stories of both good and evil, injustice, the human experience of suffering, and redemptive stories of role reversals and forgiveness. Those memories stamped upon the mind by the presence of evil, pain, and the suffering of injustice in the world need to be trained lest the sufferer lose their self to a moment.

## Training the Memory

### *Using Scripture*

THE SCRIPTURE ABOUNDS WITH stories of humanity that identify with the universal problems we face as human beings. Helping a person identify with a biblical narrative in a positive way enables their understanding of self to find health in an otherwise unpleasant circumstance. I will offer an example using the story of Ruth. Living in the Philippines it is common to see young women marry men thirty- and occasionally even forty-plus years older than they are. The book of Ruth offers them a story of redemption.

Ruth is a young woman who loves her mother in-law. Ruth's husband is deceased. Ruth and her mother in-law live in a society where land ownership is passed on to males and this practice causes the exclusion of childless women (whether barren or because they outlived their children) from the power and wealth derived through owning land.

Ruth's mother in-law is too old to attract a man, but she counsels Ruth on how to gain the attention of a wealthy older man. Naomi has no one to redeem her land and it cannot be passed onto her. Upon gaining the attention of Boaz, a wealthy landowner related to the family who can redeem the land (become the owner), Naomi counsels Ruth on the final steps of seducing the older man.

Naomi counsels Ruth to uncover Boaz and *lie down at his feet.* This phrase is a euphemism for intercourse; it seems Boaz awakens to find Ruth has already begun. The story of Ruth is a story of injustice, a widow is deprived of owning the husband's ancestral land. Her only hope is that a male relative take ownership and thereby take responsibility for Naomi and in this case Ruth also. It is a story of female seduction, of a younger woman giving her self to a man in order to preserve the life of a woman she has taken as her mother. It is not a love story. This does not mean that Ruth could not learn to love Boaz.

A subversive reality in the story of Ruth is the real identity of the kinsman redeemer. This is so because it is Ruth, a Moabite—a people of corrupt sexual mores in Israelite thought—who redeems the life of Naomi out of love. Boaz is an honorable man, but benefits from the injustice of misogynistic inheritance laws.

The story of Ruth is relatable to the Filipino woman's experience because young women marry older men for the sake of the family, of father and mother, of brother(s) and sister(s). It is further encouraging because Jesus is in the lineage of Ruth. In a crooked world, the woman who loves enough to marry an older man in order to care for her loved ones is an honorable woman.

It is notable that Scripture is primarily a collection of stories. Even the wisdom book of Job is a story. Jesus told stories and the gospels record Jesus' life as stories. The book of Acts is a collection of theologically structured stories. The Epistles enable us to enter deeper into the stories of Paul, James, Peter, and the early church. Revelation is like a fairy tale, written for those on the border of sanity, pressed by unspeakable cruelty from the oppression of empire.

## Collecting Our Own Story

How we tell our story, stories taken from our life experiences, becomes who we are, forms our personal sense of self. Storytelling trains the memory. We remember because we hear ourselves speak as we engage another person with our story, or as we write and read our own stories. A healthy person will find in their stories identity-forming lessons, identity-enforcing lessons, and a sense of providence amidst the confusion of life's absurdities.

At times life can undergo unexpected change and a person must reorient their stories to understand their evolving experience. Events like the death of a spouse, an undesired divorce, loss of health, or some other calamity all require self-reflection that enables one to move forward. Naomi and Ruth both experienced life-changing calamity and acquired new identities as they moved forward with life.

The *magic* of a story is in its flexibility. We attach ideas, emotions, beliefs, loyalties, and our own identity to stories. Yet, they can be retold with the same honesty in which they were first told, while revealing new insights related to the changing realities of life.

Our stories that we share should always be uplifting and enforce our self-worth as a member of the human family. Specifically, they should bolster our faith. Our stories should incorporate how we find God in the world. They should indicate to others how we expect to be treated. They should reveal our strengths and weaknesses. Our stories we share tell people who we've been, how we responded to life, and who we seek to become.

Forgiveness makes the world work because it is a creative force, a power that, when released, can heal the past, accept the present, and move toward hope for a better future. Forgiveness, like a story, is magic; it reorients the world to newness. Forgiveness requires a willingness to forget.

Although crimes against humanity in the course of human history must be recalled in stories and should not be forgotten, a healthy person cannot remain in the past, but must let go and seek life. They must fill their memory with new stories of ongoing life.[1]

## Forgiving and Spiritual Maturation

The administering of grace is a sign of spiritual maturation. To be merciful is to display God in public. To forgive is divine. It is the power that unleashes creation, that lifts the soul from self, that challenges us to move forward, and requires the suffering of our ego. Forgiveness releases God into our lives, into the quagmire of human relationships that become entangled in a quandary of emotions and self-justifying stories.

Forgiveness can be seemingly impossible for a trauma survivor whose soul has been intruded upon by evil. They need the loving therapy of a

---

1. Holocaust survivors and those who write about the holocaust have high rates of suicide.

community of believers who can help them produce new stories.[2] Forgiveness can be easy for the rest of us. This is so because it brings forgiveness to us and we all need to be forgiven:

> *For if ye forgive men their trespasses, your heavenly Father will also*
> *forgive you:*
> *But if ye forgive not men their trespasses, neither will your Father*
> *forgive your trespasses.*
> *(Matt 6:14–15)*

Although forgiving puts us at risk in relationship to another, it is a risk that Jesus requires us to take. This is the abiding power of a Christlike person, the willingness to risk for the sake of other human beings in need of forgiveness while recognizing their own self-justifying reasons for not doing so are inconsistent with the Spirit of the Lord:

> *Then Peter came and said to him, "Lord, if another member of the*
> *church sins against me, how often should I forgive? As many as*
> *seven times?" Jesus said to him, "Not seven times, but, I tell you,*
> *seventy-seven times.*
> *(Matt 18:21–22)*

*Forgiveness is the boundless economy of the divine presence.*

The flourishing of life is dependent upon forgiveness. Forgiveness is rooted in the belief that people can change and that in choosing to do so they receive God into their life. As human beings, we all need an environment where forgiveness is recognized as an indispensible need in order to ensure the presence of God's goodness and blessing.

*Forgiveness is the first step toward genuine reconciliation in any relationship.*

## Learning to Forget

Forgetting isn't an immediate gift. Memories aren't instantly erased. Forgetting requires a continual willingness to start over, to build again, to treat the other as God treats us: as forgiven. Forgetting is an act of faith in the

---

2. Trauma is a complex subject that cannot be addressed thoroughly in a chapter. I recommend Beste, *God and the Victim*.

Christian belief that people can be changed by forgiveness because to forgive is divine and brings God into the world.

Understanding the cost of not forgetting is imperative for learning to forget. Forgetting is a process that begins with faith; its first act is to forgive. The world doesn't work without forgiveness. Holding another person hostage with an unforgiving heart is a self-inflicting form of bondage that denigrates the Spirit of Christ.

Learning to forgive is learning to willingly choose to forget, to let go of the memories that inhibit the forward movement into newness of life. The memory arises but it is sat aside by an act of the will and not allowed to interfere with the present moment.

In the ongoing effort to justify ourselves we often recall events and expose (in our minds) the blindness of those who caused us pain. If a person is to be free from such patterns of thought and gain a sense of forgiveness they must silence such moments and choose to remember better moments. Ultimately, only the grace to forgive can heal the torment of discomfort from living in a world of failure.

Vindication isn't possible in complex human relationships, only forgiveness can correct the soul-destroying desire to be right, to be innocent. We all walk around broken in relation to someone we love, and vindication is out of reach. Recognizing that it is God who releases us from the pain of a broken relationship through our own act of forgiving others is to access the divine and all of its creative potential in the present.

*The cost of unforgiveness blackens the heart, distorts the face, and consumes possibilities for life.*

## A Parable

*The world doesn't work without forgiveness.*

A FOLLOWER OF JESUS was walking in the way of the Lord and responded to a man who sought to justify himself and exclude those members of his family who had offended him. The follower of Jesus responded, "The world doesn't work without forgiveness."

He sought further to justify himself and answered, "I've been hurt and I must protect myself." The follower of Jesus who walked in the way of the Lord responded, "Jesus was also hurt."

The man responded, "But Jesus never hurt anyone." The follower of Jesus who walked in the way of the Lord said, "Were you not born into the world the Lord made? Were you not victim to sin long before you became a perpetrator? Do you suppose yourself to be righteous beyond others? Have you not read how Jesus wrote in the sand?"

Please explain said the man. Responding, the follower of Jesus who walked in the way said, "Life is like sand and it is easy to hide one's self in the shifting sands of interpersonal relationships. It is easy to impose guilt on the other and be blind to your own. Remember, there is one who writes in the sand. For this reason, I have said that the world doesn't work without forgiveness."

# God's Merciful Culpability

**FORGIVING GOD**

*Creation limited
the self-sustaining One
His goal, a family
His existence, unmatchable
Eternity ripped at the seams
Out of God's desire, suffering was born
Love wept at possibility,
tears flowed at the cost
Could the nature of the living One be known?
Out of the blood and mud
formed and gifted with life
a family began
Children crying
People dying
Learning to be human
Feeling shame
Who is watching this mixture of life and pain?
Spirited words fill reality
An unmatchable story of love brings hope
On the lips of the suffering God
arms spread to repair eternity's rift
Comes the word
Forgive*

# God's Merciful Culpability

*God forgives us. We must forgive God for the pains of death that fill our lives, our world, all of our reality.*

I think most of us come to the place where we question God for not being more present, more helpful, and feel resentment toward God for not relieving some of the horrendous suffering that plagues history, humanity, our lives. Rather than learning to forgive God, theologians have spent vast amounts of energy on justifying God for the pain, hurt, and evil in the world. I have not found any of their attempts worthy of an adult mind.

In my thought, God desired living creatures who would be like him in an existential way, yet they could never be exactly like the omnific One. This desire of God's first appears as choice and is depicted in the speech of Lady Wisdom from Proverbs 8. It is apparent in the speech of Lady Wisdom that prior to creating, God thought about creation and made choices. In this sense it is theologically correct to say that everything flows from imagination and begins with choice.

Since there is only one self-sustaining, omnific, living being, then creation can only exist with limits. The interconnectedness of creation requires related limits in order for the universe to be more than chaotic or be useful as an external witness to God as creator (external in relation to humanity). Humanity's godlikeness is first exhibited in choice, and then image aids us along the way as we live our lives. However, we are neither the designers of the earth, nor of our own existence. This was God's doing. For this reason God can be held accountable for the human condition. The idea of holding God culpable for creation sits in contrast to the ideology of predestination, an ideology that produces an unjust God. An unjust God is not a God of love.

*It is only a radical monotheism that holds God accountable for the human condition.*

Radical monotheism simply has no place for angels and demons; they are mere personifications of powers and devices for understanding events. Job's theology resonates with a radical monotheism that holds God culpable for not being more involved in the governing of humanity.

> *The earth is given into the hand of the wicked;*
> *he covers the eyes of its judges—*
> *if it is not he, who then is it?*
> *(Job 9:24)*

# FORGIVENESS

God holds humanity accountable for their existence. God justifies this through likeness (the freedom of choice) through image (love, mercy, insight, reality-creation, naming, etc.), and finally through the moral conscience that recognizes, without special revelation, the goodness of the last six commandments of the Decalogue.

*It is easy to expose humanity's culpability for the world, for the reality we create.*

I should acknowledge that it is particularly easy to name the image-marring realities that dehumanize and destroy. Paul's vice lists and Jesus' constant warnings against greed provide us with words for humanity's corruption of reality. The Torah warns us of idols or powers that corrupt reality such as trusting in Empire, war, and ethnic pride. The prophets spoke of injustices that cause human suffering. All of these are preventable and within our power to correct, much more so for those who have received the good news of the coming of God in Jesus Christ.

*It is easy to separate God from the created order (God is not the creation).*

Because God is creator, separate from creation, then the creation is limited in the revealing of God beyond mere wondrous power. Only God's entrance into humanity, living with the limits of a human life, reveals who God is in a way complete enough for humanity to grasp the ontological nature (holiness) of God. It is faith that believes in a living God of mercy who displayed his love, his goodness, and his culpability, upon a cross. God is guilty of being merciful, guilty of love. Guilty of choosing the necessity of temporal suffering for both God's self and humanity, so that we can become the children of God. In order that God might accomplish his desire for a family, for a deified humanity to be embraced into his very being without separation, God had no other way to accomplish his desire than in the world as it is and through the story of the good news of Jesus.

*Life cannot flourish without the mercy that is always ready to forgive.*

The life and death of Jesus is both God's self-revelation and a lived display of God's culpability. With arms wide open, the God-man spoke words that challenge the theology of the church fathers; "Father, forgive them; for they do not know what they are doing" (Luke 23:34). They did not know they were murdering the Son of God, the Lord, the Incarnate Word, the Creator of all, the one God.

*Life cannot exist without forgiveness.*

In the mystery of the incarnation, God became a human being without exception. The picture is phenomenally communicative—God's culpability in his death upon a cross is fulfilled in the death of an innocent human being who exonerates humanity with a breath and God with his last.

# Bibliography

Arendt, Hannah. *Eichmann in Jerusalem: A Report on the Banality of Evil.* New York: Penguin, 1977.
Badiou, Alan. *Saint Paul: The Foundation of Universalism.* Palo Alto, CA: Stanford University Press, 2003.
Berrigan, Daniel. *To Dwell in Peace: An Autobiography.* Eugene, OR: Wipf & Stock, 2007.
Beste, Jennifer Erin. *God and the Victim: Traumatic Intrusions on Grace and Freedom.* Oxford: Oxford University Press, 2007.
Dunning, Stephen N. *Dialectical Readings: Three Types of Interpretation.* University Park, PA: Pennsylvania State University Press, 1997.
Ellul, Jacques. *Money and Power.* Basingstoke, UK: InterVarsity, 1984.
Freire, Paulo. *Pedagagy of Freedom: Ethics, Democracy and Civic Courage.* Translated by Patrick Clarke. Lanham, MD: Rowman and Littlefield, 1998.
———. *Pedagogy of the Oppressed.* Translated by Myra Bergman Ramos. New York: Continuum International, 2005.
Garner, Phillip Michael. *Interpretive Adventures: Subversive Readings in a Missional School.* Eugene, OR: Wipf & Stock, 2017.
Gill, Lesley. *The School of the Americas: Military Training and Political Violence in the Americas.* Durham, NC: Duke University Press, 2004.
Girard, Rene. *I See Satan Fall Like Lightning.* Translated by James G. Williams. Maryknoll, NY: Orbis, 2001.
Heschel, Abraham Josuha. *The Prophets.* 1st Perennial Classics ed. New York: Harper Perennial, 2001.
Johnson, Kevin R. *Mixed Race America and the Law.* New York: New York University Press, 2003.
Kaufmann, Yehezkel. *The Religion of Israel from its Beginnings to the Babylonian Exile.* Translated by Moshe Greenberg. New York: Shocken, 1960.
Kierkegaard, Søren, *The Book on Adler.* Translated by Howard V. Hong and Edna Hong. Princeton, NJ: Princeton University Press, 1998.
Linn, Brian McAllister. *The Philippine War 1899–1902.* Lawerence: University Press of Kansas, 2000.
Moon, Katherine H. S. *Sex Among Allies: Military Prostitutions in U.S.-Korea Relations.* New York: Columbia University Press, 1997.
Olson, Dennis T. *Deuteronomy and the Death of Moses: A Theological Reading.* Minneapolis: Augsburg Fortress, 1999.

BIBLIOGRAPHY

San Juan, Epifanio, Jr. *The Philippine Temptation: Dialectics of Philippines—U. S. Literary Relations.* Philadelphia: Temple University Press, 1996.

Scott, James C. *The Moral Economy of the Peasant: Rebellion and Subsistence in Southeast Asia.* London: Yale University Press, 1976.

Sobrino, Jon. *No Salvation Outside the Poor: Prophetic Utopian Essays.* Maryknoll, NY: Orbis, 2008.

Vine, David. *Base Nation: How U. S. Military Bases Abroad Harm America and the World.* New York: Metropolitan, 2015.

Weaver, Denny J. *The Nonviolent Atonement.* Grand Rapids: Eerdmans, 2001.

Zinn, Howard. *A People's History of the United States.* New York: Harper Collins, 2003.

Made in the USA
Columbia, SC
06 April 2023

14987037R00107